Library of
Davidson College

PACCA SERIES ON THE DOMESTIC ROOTS OF UNITED STATES FOREIGN POLICY

Rules of the Game

American Politics and the Central America Movement

JOSHUA COHEN AND JOEL ROGERS

Rules of the Game

American Politics and the Central America Movement

**PACCA SERIES ON THE DOMESTIC ROOTS OF
U.S. FOREIGN POLICY**

Rules of the Game:
American Politics and
the Central America Movement

Joshua Cohen and Joel Rogers

South End Press   Boston, MA

Copyright © 1986 by Joshua Cohen and Joel Rogers

Copyrights are still required for book production in the United States. However, in our case, it is a disliked necessity. Thus, any properly footnoted quotation of up to 500 sequential words may be used without permission, as long as the total number of words quoted does not exceed 2000. For longer quotations or for a greater number of words quoted, written permission from the publisher is required.

First edition
Typesetting by South End Press
Layout and Production by Mike Prokosch and Elizabeth Stahl
Manufactured in the USA

Library of Congress Cataloguing in Publication Data

Cohen, Joshua, 1951-
The rules of the game
1. Central America—Foreign relations—United States.   2. United States—Foreign relations—Central America.   3. United States—Politics and government—1981-   4. Political parties—United States—History—20th century.   I. Rogers, Joel, 1952-   II. Title.
F1436.8.U6C64   1986   320.973   86-21918
ISBN 0-89608-326-8

SOUTH END PRESS   116 St. Botolph St.   BOSTON, MA 02115

Domestic Roots Statement

Domestic Roots of U.S. Foreign Policy is a project of Policy Alternatives for the Caribbean and Central America (PACCA), an association of scholars and policymakers. Through research, analysis, policy recommendations, and the collaboration of analysts in the U.S. and the Caribbean Basin, PACCA aims to promote a humane and democratic alternative to present U.S. policies toward Central America and the Caribbean.

The principles of such an alternative are set forth in PACCA's *Changing Course: Blueprint for Peace in Central America and the Caribbean:*

> U.S. foreign policy should be based on the principles which it seeks to further in the world. These include: non-intervention, respect for self-determination, collective self-defense, peaceful settlement of disputes, respect for human rights, support for democratic development and concern for democratic values. Adherence to these principles is critical to working out practical programs for regional peace and development.

Participants in the *Domestic Roots* project endorse these principles, and seek to widen discussion of alternative policies based on them. The project explores the links between current U.S. policies in the region and major institutions and issues in U.S. domestic politics. In a series of pamphlets, *Domestic Roots* will highlight the continuity between domestic policy initiatives and current policies in the region, locate the domestic sources of current policy choices there, and assess the obstacles to and opportunities for widening debate about those policies, and constructing a decent and democratic alternative to them.

PACCA Executive Board

Robert Armstrong, North American Congress on Latin America
Roger Burbach, Center for the Study of the Americas
Joseph Collins, Institute for Food and Development Policy
Michael Conroy, University of Texas
Carmen Diana Deere, University of Massachusetts
Richard R. Fagen, Stanford University
Xabier Gorostiaga, Regional Office for Economic and Social Research, Managua
Nora Hamilton, University of Southern California
Saul Landau, Institute for Policy Studies
William LeoGrande, American University

Domestic Roots Project

Robert Armstrong, North American Congress on Latin America; PACCA Executive Board
Joshua Cohen, Massachusetts Institute of Technology
Frances Fox Piven, City University of New York
Joel Rogers, University of Miami
Juliet Schor, Harvard University; Center for Popular Economics
Mark Tushnet, Georgetown University Law Center

PACCA Executive Director: Robert Stark
       Outreach Staff: Joy Hackel
       Publications Editor: Colin Danby

PACCA
1506 19th Street, N.W.
Washington, D.C. 20036
202-332-6333

The people who *own* the country *ought to govern it.*

—John Jay

Table of Contents

Introduction	1
1. American Exceptionalism: The Politics of Fragmentation	4
Constitutional Design	5
Geography and Natural Resources	7
Uneven Economic Development	9
Racism	11
Ethnic and Religious Divisions	13
State Repression	14
2. Conventional Politics: Parties and Voting	17
Parties	19
Just Two Parties	20
Party Weakness and Failure	22
Voting	24
3. Right Turn: American Politics in the 1980s	30
The Decline of Labor	31
The Collapse of the New Deal System	35
The New Party System	38
The Democrats	40
4. Changing Course? The Constraints of Present Politics	44
The Importance of Strategy	45
All Strategies Have Costs	46
Working With the Democrats	49
The Importance of an Alternative	51
Attitudes	53
Notes	55
Resources	58

Tables

Table 1: Taxing and Spending: Taxes and Elementary and Secondary School Expenditures, Selected States	7
Table 2: Two Americas?	12
Table 3: Major Third Parties in American History	21
Table 4: Who Shapes U.S. Foreign Policy?	32
Table 5: The Internationalization of the U.S. Economy	37
Table 6: Presidential Requests and Congressional Appropriations for the Military Budget, Fiscal Years 1980-85	40

Figures

Figure 1: Territorial Expansion of the United States	8
Figure 2: Voter Turnout in the U.S. Compared to Other Countries	23
Figure 3: Turnout in Presidential Elections: 1824-1980	25
Figure 4: The Decline of Organized Labor	34
Figure 5: Political Party Receipts, 1975-82	39

Boxes

Box 1: Uneven Economic Development	10
Box 2: State Repression: A Thing of the Past?	15
Box 3: Rational Ignorance?	18
Box 4: Realignment, Dealignment, and the Importance of Parties	26
Box 5: The Growing Presidential Role in Foreign Policy	33

Acknowledgements

For comments, criticisms, and advice, we thank Robert Armstrong, Robert Borosage, Stephen Bronner, Roger Burbach, Susana Cepeda, Colin Danby, Joy Hackel, Saul Landau, William LeoGrande, Cynthia Peters, Frances Fox Piven, Debra Reuben, Juliet Schor, Terri Shuck, Angela Sanbrano, Frank Solowey, Robert Stark, Mark Tushnet, and Jenny Yancey. For their help in designing and producing this pamphlet, we thank Mike Prokosch and Elizabeth Stahl.

Cambridge and Miami J.C. and J.R.
July 30, 1986

Introduction

Politics is hard. Changing the course of government policies is harder still. Anyone who has ever engaged in conventional political action—whether by working on a campaign, or lobbying a Representative or Senator, or registering people to vote—knows this. It is very difficult to see results from one's actions, or even link them in any meaningful way to the actions of others.

Often this is true even when popular majorities oppose the policies of the government. Public opinion polls, for example, indicate that most Americans oppose social spending cutbacks, business deregulation, and high levels of unemployment. But these have been the core of the Reagan administration's domestic program. Most Americans also favor arms control with the Soviet Union, and oppose the magnitude of the Reagan military buildup. Here too there are striking gaps between public opinion and public policy, gaps which underscore the difficulty of translating unorganized opinion into political power.[1]

Such difficulties are particularly frustrating for those who seek to move public policies in a more democratic direction. Consider the dilemma faced by critics of U.S. policies toward Central America. Over the last two decades the American public has become more sceptical of the use of military force abroad. As late as 1965, after more than a decade of military and technical assistance, the installation of thousands of military advisers, and even the commitment of tens of thousands of American ground troops, popular opposition to America's war on Vietnam was just beginning to emerge. Today, with a much lower level of U.S. "involvement," strong majorities of Americans, and even a majority of those who approve of the job Ronald Reagan is doing as President, oppose aid to the Nicaraguan contras.[2] But while widespread public disagreement with present policies has slowed their development, it has not reversed them. Once again, something seems to be blocking the transmission of policy choices from the people to their government.

This pamphlet is based on the belief that an important part of that blockage is the system of conventional politics itself. In a variety of ways, we will argue, the American political system tends to constrain popular democratic action. Some of these constraints are part of the basic *structure* of the American state and society. Others result from the *organization* of party politics and voting in the U.S. And still others derive from the recent changes in the *content* of party politics and public policy signalled by the "Reagan revolution." In this, the second pamphlet in the *Domestic Roots* series, we examine this system of multiple and overlapping constraints on democratic action.

Rules of the Game has four parts:

Part 1 analyzes the strikingly fragmented (decentralized and uncoordinated) character of politics in the U.S. We argue that a variety of deeply rooted features of the U.S.—including basic constitutional design, geography and natural resources, uneven economic development, racism, ethnic diversity, and state repression—all contribute to this fragmentation, which in turn raises enormous barriers to popular politics. In effect, the political system makes it difficult for individuals of ordinary means to unite in opposition to those with greater wealth.

Part 2 considers how political fragmentation is reflected in and advanced through the organization of party politics and voting. We focus on the organizational weakness and non-ideological character of the two major parties, and on the barriers to the formation of third parties. The discussion of voting centers on the relatively low levels of participation in the U.S., and the ways that electoral participation varies across social groups. One phenomenon highlighted by the argument is that the most natural constituency for democratic change in America—those who are poor, and not benefitting from the present arrangements of power—is also the least active.

Part 3 explores the collapse of the New Deal party system, and the changes in public policy that have followed on that collapse. The discussion concentrates on the decline of the Democratic Party, which was centrally identified with the New Deal, and which, of the two major parties, is the more likely arena for discussion of democratic alternatives to present policies.

Most of the analysis in Parts 1-3 is general. We believe it has relevance for critics of *any* current policies, foreign or domestic. But we are particularly concerned with changing the course of U.S. policies toward Central America and the Caribbean. Part 4 therefore concludes our discussion with a consideration of how these various constraints affect the choices and opportunities of those who oppose those policies, and wish to work for a democratic alternative to them.

Before beginning the discussion, three general points about our purposes and argument should be noted.

Introduction

First, we are interested in widening public debate about U.S. public policy, both by widening the range of that debate and widening the range of participants in it. We write this pamphlet in the belief that understanding more about the *barriers* to such democratization can contribute to achieving it. Among other things, we believe that a greater understanding of the *constraints* on democratic action can help to illuminate the difficult strategic *choices* that democratic critics must always make.

To be sure, any sustained examination of the obstacles to popular democratic action risks being one-sided. By emphasizing obstacles, it may obscure the long history of popular struggles against those obstacles, and miss the important lessons those struggles hold for activists today. (A future *Domestic Roots* pamphlet on social movements in the U.S. will examine this history, and what might be learned from it.) The risk, however, appears worth taking. Success in breaking down the barriers to popular action requires a realistic appraisal of those barriers themselves.

Second, we emphasize that "illuminating" strategic questions is not the same as answering them. The analysis offered here helps to explain certain features of political organization in the U.S. It indicates, for example, how the structure of the political system tends to fragment opposition, why political participation is very low, and why the parties are as unresponsive as they commonly are to movements in public opinion. Understanding such things may help inform and sharpen political judgments. But when all is said and done, hard political choices will still have to be made. Reasonable people with like aspirations will come to different conclusions about these choices. No analysis can change that fact. This one does not pretend to.

Third and finally, we believe that if the basic structure of American politics did not fragment and discourage popular politics, public policies would be *better*. In addition to being a more democratic country, featuring wider participation and debate, the U.S. would also be a saner and more humane one. Its policies toward Central America and the Caribbean, for example, would be less murderous and cruel. In short, we believe that the pursuit of democracy at home is the best hope for achieving decent public policies at home and abroad.

1. American Exceptionalism: The Politics of Fragmentation

The essence of politics is collective action—different people acting together for the achievement of common aims. There are many conditions for such action—including common interests, an awareness of those interests, a willingness to cooperate with one another, and the ability to sustain the costs of that cooperation.

On all these dimensions and others, the structure of the U.S. political system tends to constrain collective action by people of ordinary means. Most importantly, *American political conflict and bargaining is extremely fragmented*. Instead of bringing people together, the basic structures of American politics tend to keep them separate and divided, while encouraging the pursuit of narrower interests. This division raises the costs of coordination. Its effects are most sharply pronounced among those who have few resources to begin with—that is, among those whose "strength is in numbers," and not in their wallets.

Reflecting these tendencies to fragmentation, ordinary people in the U.S. are among the most politically disorganized in the world. Most strikingly, perhaps, the U.S. is virtually unique among advanced industrial capitalist democracies in never having had a labor party or socialist movement of significant strength and duration. To this day, conventional political debate here is not marked by the sort of class-based cleavages and terms ("workers" versus "capitalists") characteristic of the political systems of Italy, France, Germany, England, and indeed most of advanced industrial world. This peculiar absence of class politics in the U.S.—one instance of the general fragmentation of the U.S. political system—is called "American exceptionalism."[3]

In Part 2 we return to the consequences of political fragmentation and "American exceptionalism," considering how they are reflected in the organizations of conventional politics. Here, however, we address the prior question: What generates these conditions in the first place? As might be expected, the answer is that over the course of U.S. history many factors have contributed, and that the importance of particular factors, and their interaction with others, has shifted over the course of U.S. history. Such historical variation and political complexity pose severe problems in providing an adequate rendering of American exceptionalism—problems which, we should emphasize, we do not pretend to solve here. These important complexities aside, however, there are six basic factors which can be identified as having contributed throughout *all* of U.S. history. Reinforcing one another, and given varied political expression, they have always been central to producing, and reproducing, the politics of fragmentation.

Constitutional Design

The basic founding document of the United States, the Constitution, mandates a fragmented government structure. This has permitted, within a single nation, considerable political experimentation, particularly at the local level, and has helped ensure certain limits on the abuse of centralized powers. But the clear effect of constitutional fragmentation has also been to limit the potential for political cooperation among people of ordinary means, and this was something that the architects of the constitutional system, the "founding fathers," clearly recognized and desired.

In *The Federalist Papers,* for example, James Madison explained that a fragmented system would help cure "the mischiefs of faction," whose most common source was the distribution of property ownership:

> Those who hold and those who are without property have ever formed distinct interests in society. Those who are creditors, and those who are debtors, fall under a like discrimination... The regulation of these various and interfering interests forms the principal task of modern legislation and involves the spirit of party and faction in the necessary and ordinary operations of government.[4]

Madison was particularly concerned that a "majority faction" composed of those owning little property might come together to challenge inequalities in wealth and income. He saw two ways to prevent its formation:

> Either the existence of the same passion or interest in a majority at the same time must be prevented, or the majority, having such coexistent passion or interest, must be rendered, by their number and local situation, unable to concert and carry into effect schemes of oppression.[5]

In the constitutional scheme they eventually agreed upon, Madison and the other framers accordingly sought both to prevent majorities from forming common programs, and to impose barriers to the implementation of those programs, should they be formed. The most straightforward way this was done was by weakening and dividing the American state.

The Constitution, for example, mandates a *separation of powers* at the national level. The legislative, executive, and judicial functions are each assigned to distinct branches of government, and each branch is given powers to block the activities of the other two. While the power of the judiciary to curtail Congressional or Presidential action is great, probably the most important separation and source of blockage is that between executive and legislative authority. In contrast to parliamentary systems of representation, where the leader of the dominant party (or coalition of parties) in the legislature is also the chief executive of government, the U.S. Constitution mandates separate elections for Congress and the Presidency. This has commonly meant, as is currently the case, that the President comes from a party that does not command a majority within the legislature. Such differences between the executive and the legislature typically generate barriers to concerted national policy—except of course in those cases (foreign affairs being the source of most examples) where "bipartisan consensus" obtains between the major parties.

Additionally limiting the effectiveness of the national government, and limiting the potential for the emergence of majoritarian factions, is the principle of *federalism*. This means that public power is shared between the national government and the states. By contrast with "unified" governments, where subnational units are extensions of a central authority, the United States is a "divided" government, in which the states enjoy powers independent of the Federal government. Competing with the Federal government and one another, the 50 states produce wide variations in policy on basic issues, and reinforce political diversity and division (see Table 1).

Even within national government, moreover, federalism shapes the perspective and interests of Congress. Candidates for Congress are not selected by national parties, but by state and local organizations. Members are then elected by local constituencies, and to stay in Congress they must satisfy the interests of those constituencies. Local interests are thus represented both in state governments and the national legislature. In fact, aside from the Presidency (and even there the case is ambiguous), there is no Federal office or body whose members are selected by exclusively national criteria. As House Speaker Tip O'Neill often points out, in the U.S. *"all politics is local politics."*

One effect of this is to immensely complicate the consideration of national issues, and to introduce yet additional barriers in generating coherent national policies. A closely related effect is the *discouragement* of attempts at such national coordination, and the *encouragement* of a local or regional orientation in political action. This orientation, in turn, tends to solidify differences and divisions among people located in different places.

Table 1: Taxing and Spending: Taxes and Elementary and Secondary School Expenditures, Selected States

	State	State Taxes Per Capita 1983 (in $)	Expenditures Per Pupil 1985 (in $)
Low	Arizona	771	2,344
	Tennessee	803	2,349
	Alabama	806	2,241
Middle	Kansas	1,129	3,668
	Vermont	1,138	3,783
	Nebraska	1,146	3,128
High	New York	1,889	5,226
	Wyoming	2,443	4,809
	Alaska	4,908	6,867

Source: U.S. Bureau of the Census, **Statistical Abstract of the United States 1986,** 106th ed. (Washington, DC: GPO, 1986), Tables 233, 455.

Geography and Natural Resources

In comparative terms, the United States has always been an enormous country, larger at its founding than all other countries of the time except Russia, and today, more than 200 years later, still larger than all countries but the Soviet Union, Canada, and China. Early on, the framers recognized that sheer size, like constitutional divisions, would tend to impose barriers to the existence and formation of mischievous majority factions. Rejecting the received wisdom in political theory, *The Federalist Papers* extolled the virtues of a "large commercial republic." Size would encourge a diversity of interests, and that diversity would in turn pose barriers to the existence and coordination of any stable popular majority.

In addition to encouraging diversity, the great size of the land, which for long periods had an open frontier, helped to provide a safety valve for social unrest. Those who did not like it in one place—and were not slaves—could simply leave. The widespread availability of free or very cheap land, moreover, facilitated widespread land *ownership.* This helped confirm Americans' status as a race of independent and free (white) men, and provided a ballast of popular support for a private property regime.

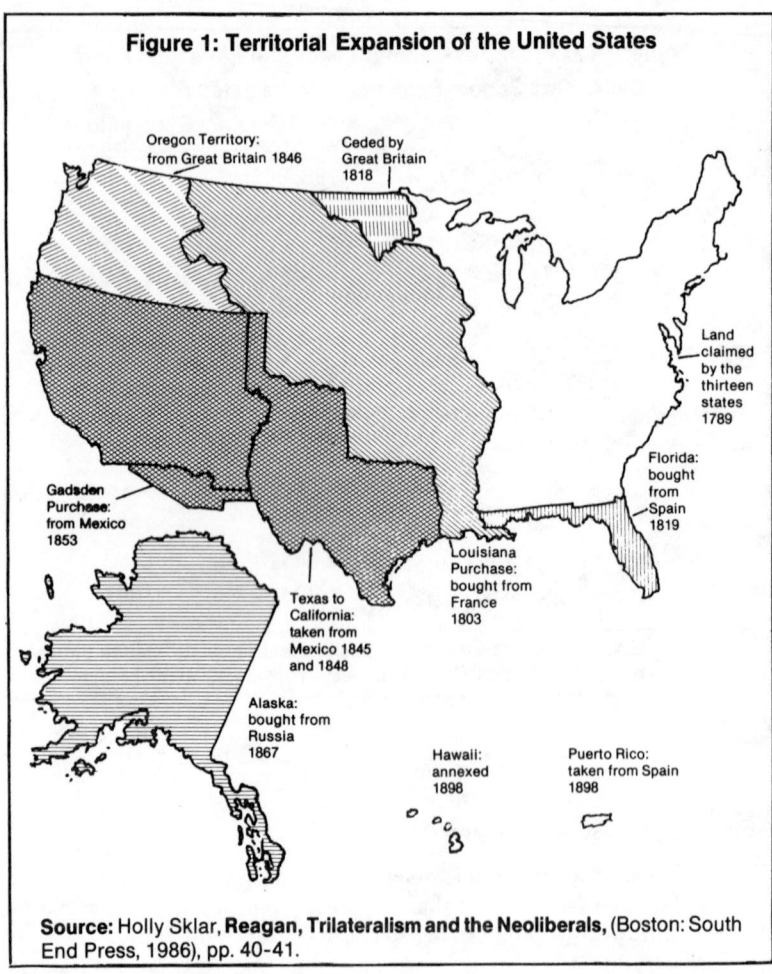

Source: Holly Sklar, **Reagan, Trilateralism and the Neoliberals,** (Boston: South End Press, 1986), pp. 40-41.

The repeated acquisition of new land helped prolong the period of an open frontier (see Figure 1). Even after the rate of acquisition slowed, however, and even after the frontier was closed, the U.S. would also enjoy comparatively low population densities. Combined with the sheer size of the country, the sparse settlement of the land in turn meant that its different inhabitants could afford to operate in relative isolation from one another. This in turn encouraged extremely diverse, and largely uncoordinated, forms of political organization, giving further substance to the constitutional fragmentation of American politics.[6]

Political fragmentation was also encouraged by America's strategic isolation. For most of its history—at least from the peace with Britain that concluded the War of 1812 to the Japanese attack on Pearl Harbor in 1941—the U.S. enjoyed a long unbroken period of strategic isolation, during which thousands of miles of ocean provided a bar to credible attack from abroad. It could thus develop without much concern for the activities of other nations, and could afford the highly decentralized political system that more threatened nations could not.

Finally, in addition to being big and isolated, the U.S. enjoyed (and continues to enjoy) tremendous advantages of climate and natural resources. Even leaving aside the productive activities of men and women, it is truly the richest nation on earth. Virtually all of the country is located in the temperate zone, which is ideal for agriculture and industry. Early settlers found vast desposits of timber and basic minerals, some of the best farmland on earth, apparently limitless water resources for farming and industry, and extended systems of lakes and rivers that eased the flow of trade. Once these resources were taken from their Native American owners, this was an almost perfect setting for economic development, which proceeded quickly.

By providing the basis for a comparatively high standard of living, these natural endowments tended to discourage efforts at collective organization along class lines. Throughout almost all of American history, and even after they had changed from a race of independent farmers to a population of wage and salary workers, ordinary people in the U.S. were paid more, and lived far better, than their counterparts in Western Europe and the rest of the developed world. In this relatively affluent environment, and especially given all the other social and political incentives to seek private gains, the appeal of collective organization was diminished. As the German economist Werner Sombart once overstated the point, "Socialist utopias came to nothing on roast beef and apple pie."[7]

Uneven Economic Development

The very rapid emergence of the U.S. as a major economic power concealed tremendous differences within the U.S. in the level and scope of economic activity. It was only after the Civil War that capitalism was firmly established as the exclusive mode of economic production in the U.S., and only after World War II, with the industrial development of the South, that it was possible to speak of a truly national industrial economy. This unevenness, combined with the tremendous diversity of American economic activity, encouraged different and competing interests in different regions of the country. An incalculably large part of American politics—from immigration to energy policy—is and always has been concerned with managing these differences.

Like so many other dynamics of American politics, this phenomenon of regional diversity was most dramatically highlighted by the Civil War. In that effort, infant industry and finance in the Northeast and Midwest joined with independent farming interests to crush the plantation South, initiating a period of economic and political subordination that would last well into

> **Box 1: Uneven Economic Development**
>
> One way of indicating regional disparities in economic development in the U.S. is to compare the average income per person in different regions of the country to the national average. For the sake of convenience, here we always set the national average at 100. Thus a region with a per capita income twice the national average will be at 200, while one with half the national average will be at 50. We examine four regions over the period 1840-1970. The regions are: Middle Atlantic (comprising the states of New York, New Jersey, Pennsylvania, Delaware, Maryland, and the District of Columbia); South Atlantic (Virginia, West Virginia, North Carolina, Georgia, and Florida); East South Central (Kentucky, Tennessee, Alabama, and Mississippi); and Pacific (Washington, Oregon, and California).
>
> | Year | US | Middle Atlantic | South Atlantic | East South Central | Pacific |
> | --- | --- | --- | --- | --- | --- |
> | 1970 | ·100 | 113 | 86 | 74 | 110 |
> | 1965 | 100 | 114 | 81 | 71 | 115 |
> | 1960 | 100 | 116 | 77 | 67 | 118 |
> | 1950 | 100 | 116 | 74 | 63 | 121 |
> | 1940 | 100 | 124 | 69 | 55 | 138 |
> | 1930 | 100 | 140 | 56 | 48 | 130 |
> | 1920 | 100 | 134 | 59 | 52 | 135 |
> | 1900 | 100 | 139 | 45 | 49 | 163 |
> | 1880 | 100 | 141 | 45 | 51 | 204 |
> | 1840 | 100 | 136 | 70 | 73 | --- |
>
> **Source:** U.S. Bureau of the Census, **Historical Statistics of the United States: Colonial Times to 1970** (Washington, DC: GPO, 1976), Series F 287-296.
>
> The table indicates that regional disparities have substantially decreased in the past few decades. But it also shows that substantial disparities remain, and that for long periods of American history some regions were 3, 4, or more times more wealthy than others. In particular, note the long economic backwardness of the Deep South.

the 20th century. The long deflation that followed the war (like most major wars, it had been paid for by printing money) eventually ignited the great agrarian protest movement of the Populists, which drew particular strength from independent farmers in the South, Midwest, and West. But within a generation of the close of the war predominantly Northeastern industrial and financial interests had crushed the Populists as well, and were busy rolling back political organization, and even electoral participation, among the dependent classes.[8]

Such dramatic events aside, and even after the great levelling of regional differences that has occurred over the past 40 years, uneven and diverse economic development tends to fragment U.S. politics. Among elites, the enduring vitality of regional splits is evident in phenomena like the "Sagebrush Rebellion," which pits Western business interests against the Northeast in a battle over environmental regulation and Federal land management in the West. Among non-elites, it is evident in the difficulties northern workers have encountered from their southern counterparts in responding to "runaway" shops down South. Regional economic differences continue to slow concerted national responses to problems, and to divide ordinary people with potentially shared interests from one another.

Racism

The first black slaves were brought to America in the early 1600s. By the time of the Declaration of Independence in 1776, slavery was established in all thirteen colonies. Oppressive relations between whites and blacks in America are as old as the country itself.

The history since is familiar, or should be. Shortly after the Revolution, the "First Emancipation" began in New England, as state after state abolished slavery, or phased it out. The most substantial black populations, however, were located in the South, and this "emancipation" stopped at Virginia. Growing tensions between the slave and non-slave states, which were importantly tensions between a precapitalist plantation economy and the imperatives of free capitalist development, eventually erupted in the Civil War. Ostensibly the war freed the slaves, but with the collapse of "radical" efforts to reconstruct the South in the postwar period, an elaborate system of oppressive and segregationist race relations was soon reestablished.

It would not be until well into the twentieth century—when the combined push of the mechanization of southern agriculture, and the pull of labor-starved northern industry in World War II, brought millions of blacks north—that racism began to be seriously addressed on a national scale. And it would not be until the 1960s, and only then under the pressures of massive protest and civil disobedience, that the major legal components of discrimination would be broken down. The fight over *de facto* discrimination—in housing, education, employment, and other essentials—continues, and blacks and whites in this country continue to live very different sorts of lives (see Table 2).

Volumes have been written on American racism. Suffice it to say here that there is no more persistent form of division in American politics, and none more debilitating to popular democratic politics. In the pre-Civil War period, the small number of "freedmen" who trickled North were almost universally excluded from early worker organizations. In the late 19th

Table 2: Two Americas?		
	White	Black
Median household net worth, 1984	$39,135	$3,397
Percent of households with zero or negative net worth, 1984	8.4%	30.5%
Poverty rate, 1984	11.5%	33.8%
Poverty rate for children under 18, 1984	16.5%	46.5%
Infant mortality rate (deaths per 1,000 births), 1982	10.1	19.6
Median family income, 1984	$27,686	$15,432
Unemployment rate, 1985	6.2%	15.1%
Percent of families headed by a single man, 1984	3.0%	5.3%
Percent of families headed by a single woman, 1984	12.6%	43.1%
Male murder rate (deaths by homicide per 100,000), 1982	9.6	59.1
Female murder rate, 1982	3.1	12.0
Percent expressing "satisfaction with the way things are going in the U.S. at this time," Sept., 1984	52%	16%
Percent expressing "dissatisfaction with the way things are going in the U.S. at this time," Sept. 1984	42%	74%
Percent voting for Ronald Reagan, 1984	66%	9%

Sources: **New York Times,** 19 July 1986; U.S. Bureau of Census, **Current Population Reports,** Series P-60, No. 149, **Money Income and Poverty Status of Families and Persons in the U.S.: 1984** (Washington, DC: GPO, 1985), Tables A, B; **Statistical Abstract,** Tables 57, 113, 287; **Economic Report of the President, 1986** (Washington, D.C.: GPO, 1986), Table B-35; **The Gallup Poll: Public Opinion 1984** (Wilmington, DE: Scholarly Resources, 1985), 208; **New York Times** /CBS News Poll, **New York Times,** 8 November 1984.

century, each of the great attempts at forging class-wide ties in labor failed to confront the race question, giving force to endless employer strategies of "divide and conquer" between antagonistic racial groups. In the 20th century, at the peak of worker organization immediately after World War II, the failure to press the issue of racial equality by organizing the South defined the limits of labor's national power for a generation, and hastened its decline. And even today, 120 years after the close of the Civil War, racial animosity and fear, and the forms and habits of political association based on them, continue to impede the construction of a truly popular democratic coalition. The racial and ethnic tensions which marked the Rainbow Coalition's effort in 1984, to take only the most recent major example, provide ample evidence on this point.

Ethnic and Religious Divisions

At least until the turn of the 20th century, the great natural wealth of the U.S., along with its rapid economic development and low population density, produced chronic labor shortages. The solution to this problem was provided by immigrant labor.

Over 1820-1830, only a little over 150,000 immigrants came to the U.S. Three decades later, over 1851-60, the inflow had risen to 2.6 million. By 1881-90, as the U.S. entered a peak phase in industrialization, the number doubled to 5.2 million. And at its high point, over 1901-10, it rose to 8.7 million, or better than 10 percent of the resident population. In today's terms, that would amount to roughly 25 million new workers over the course of the 1980s.[9]

Given all the other constraints on popular action, the fact that the population of the U.S. was comprised of people from diverse cultural backgrounds—while surely one of the appealing features of American society—contributed to the general fragmentation of U.S. politics and the weakness of worker organization within it. Coming to a vast land, with a decentralized political structure, successive waves of immigrants took up residence in communities that were often isolated from one another, and developed political commitments and organizations peculiar to individual locales. The deeply ethnic character of much local American politics—Slavs in the Midwest, Irish in Boston, Jews in New York—can be traced to this experience. The fact that the system was sufficiently porous and diffuse to permit such localized expressions, in turn, tended to consolidate patterns of organizational isolation along ethnic grounds. The myth of the American "melting pot" was only that—a myth. In all sorts of ways, immigrants found that they could preserve ethnic identities in the new land. But the maintenance of these diverse identities also tended to undermine attempts to forge alliances among workers that cut across ethnic differences.

Complementing the barriers of language and custom, and immensely important throughout American politics, were the deep religious splits with which ethnic divisions were commonly associated. In part because Americans never had to struggle for land or political rights against an entrenched church, the U.S. has always been a deeply religious country, and throughout its history religion has often served as an organizing metaphor for political action. Popular support for the Revolutionary War, for example, was fueled by the "First Great Awakening" of Protestant religious fervor; and black churches have long supplied the backbone of struggles for civil rights.

Even more often, however, religious differences have served to undermine or distort popular democratic politics. The arrival of waves of Irish

Catholic immigrants in the 1850s, for example, led to the nativist backlash of the "Know Nothing" movement, and helped trigger the realignment of political parties that issued in the modern Republican and Democratic parties. This divided workers along Protestant/Catholic lines, reflected not only in the parties but in all manner of popular organizations. And just as the U.S. was entering the second great phase of industrialization in the late 19th century, a tidal wave of new immigrants from southern and eastern Europe introduced yet additional divisions into emergent worker organizations. Ably exploited by employers, ethnic and religious cleavages repeatedly wrecked efforts at working class solidarity.[10]

State Repression

Despite the many structural barriers to their coordination, ordinary Americans have often banded together to attempt to improve their condition. With some rare and notable exceptions, these efforts have met with physical violence, imprisonment, brutally applied court sanctions, or more subtle forms of harassment and intimidation sponsored by the state. Such state repression makes for a long history, coextensive with the history of the United States. It runs roughly from the 1786 suppression of the protests of indebted farmers in Massachusetts (Shay's Rebellion), through the labor injunctions that helped wreck worker organizations in the late 19th century, to the Reagan administration's current surveillance of Central America activists, and prosecution of church groups offering sanctuary to refugees from U.S. policies in that region.

Over the last two hundred years, there have been too many government sponsored shootings, beatings, lynchings, police spies, agents provocateurs, goons, scabs, rigged trials, imprisonments, burglaries, and illegal wiretaps to permit easy summary here.[11] Once again we only note the obvious. By raising the costs of political action to individuals—in money, physical pain, imprisonment, or the destruction of their personal lives—repression makes it less likely that individuals will be willing to engage in collective political activity at all. And this is especially true for those individuals, comprising the most obvious mischievous faction, who can least afford those costs, since they have little "property" or other resources of their own.

Over the course of U.S. history, these six basic factors—constitutional design, geography and natural resources, uneven economic development, racism, ethnic and religious divisions, and state repression—have repeatedly constrained popular democratic action in the U.S. As indicated earlier, appreciating the interaction of these different factors at different times would require discussion of the peculiarities of particular circumstances and periods, and of the ways in which these divisions were themselves institutionalized and given political expression. This, again, we cannot do here. What is important to recognize, however, is that these sources of divisions are enduring and ongoing features of U.S. politics, and not merely of historical interest. They operate now, as well as having operated in the past.

Box 2: State Repression: A Thing of the Past?

The number of state-sanctioned lynchings in the U.S. has long since declined, and it is more difficult now than it was in the 1920s to deport "undesirable" aliens without due process. Still, it is a mistake to think of state interference with basic civil rights and liberties as a thing of the distant past.

To take a recent example of widespread state repression, consider government activities during the Vietnam War. During that period, separate programs of domestic spying and surveillance were directed against opponents of the war by the Federal Bureau of Investigation (COINTELPRO), the Central Intelligence Agency (Operations CHAOS, Merrimac, and Resistance), the National Security Agency (Operation MINARET), the Internal Revenue Service, Army Intelligence, and the Nixon White House itself.

As part of CHAOS, for example, over 1967-73 the CIA gathered 10,000 files on scores of individuals and more than 100 political organizations. Operation MINARET, initiated by the NSA in 1967, involved direct monitoring of international telephone and cable traffic of U.S. citizens; in response to requests from the FBI, CIA, Army Intelligence, and other agencies, it intercepted messages from more than 1600 individuals and groups, and delivered more than 1100 pages of material to Operation CHAOS. The FBI's COINTELPRO operations—which aimed to instigate conflict within and between groups, to destroy the reputations of individuals, and to prevent targeted individuals and groups from meeting and speaking—were directed against, among others, the Communist Party, the Socialist Workers Party, a wide variety of black organizations, and the "New Left." Some 200 COINTELPRO operations were conducted in 1969 alone. A staff report prepared for the Senate Intelligence Committee later described COINTELPRO as "a political vigilante operation aimed squarely at preventing the exercise of First Amendment rights of speech and association."

The Nixon White House's own programs of spying and disruption added to these activities, and underscored the enormous discretion of the government in choosing its targets. An August 1971 memo from White House counsel John Dean explained that the purpose of the famous Nixon "enemies lists" was to put in motion the "available federal machinery to screw our political enemies" in such areas as "grant availability, federal contracts, litigation, prosecution, etc." Targets for such "screwing" ranged from such apolitical celebrities as Joe Namath, to the guests at a dinner honoring labor leader Victor Reuther, to one individual whose only apparent "crime" was a $1 donation to the Presidential campaign of Maine Senator Edmund Muskie.

Source: Frank Donner, **The Age of Surveillance** (New York: Knopf, 1980); Goldstein, **Political Repression** (see footnote 11).

And part of the reason for this, as we shall see now, is that they are continually reproduced through the *organization* of politics in the U.S.

2. U.S. Conventional Politics: Parties and Voting

If the essence of politics is collective action, the essence of popular politics is *organization.* Any capitalist society (or indeed any society relying on material incentives to production) features inequalities in the distribution of material resources. Such material inequalities tend, in turn, to generate political inequalities; they make wealthy individuals far more powerful than poor ones. Organization is so important to popular politics because it can reduce these political consequences of background inequalities. Organization permits individuals to pool their resources, and thus to share the costs of collective action. For those who have few resources to begin with, organization is the precondition of political power.

To see the force of this point, consider a familiar problem of collective action: the problem of information. Everyone would agree that without information, political activity is unguided and ineffective. But given scarce resources, and assuming that their action will not be coordinated with the actions of others, it seldom makes sense for individual citizens to inform themselves even about major issues of public policy. The reason is that the costs of acquiring information will almost always be greater than the expected benefit of acting on that information, *so long as individuals act in isolation from one another.* Since even under the best of circumstances a single vote will not make much difference in policy outcomes, it is more sensible to adopt a position of "rational ignorance," and limit one's information about policy choices to that which can be acquired for "free" from lobbyists, advertisers, and the like. This information is only supplied for "free," however, because of the benefits its suppliers expect from providing it.

It can thus be expected that this information is *biased* toward the interests of the individuals and groups that provide it—individuals and

> **Box 3: Rational Ignorance?**
>
> As the text indicates, in the absence of strong political organizations it seldom makes sense for individual voters of ordinary means to inform themselves about issues of public policy. While the problem cannot be blamed entirely on weak political organizations in the U.S., it is true that American voters are profoundly uninformed about basic issues of public policy, and even the basic structure of the political system. A **New York Times**/CBS Poll in April 1986, for example, indicated that only 38% of Americans even know which side the U.S. is currently supporting in Nicaragua—the contras or the government. As the chart below indicates, this lack of knowledge about issues is not new, or limited to the Central America case.
>
> | Percent of Americans | Who... | Year |
> |---|---|---|
> | 70 | Can name their mayor | 1967 |
> | 69 | Know which party has most members in U.S. House of Representatives | 1978 |
> | 68 | Know that President is limited to two terms | 1970 |
> | 52 | Know that there are two U.S. Senators from their state | 1978 |
> | 46 | Can name their U.S. Representative | 1973 |
> | 39 | Can name both U.S. Senators from their state | 1973 |
> | 38 | Know the U.S.S.R. is not a NATO member | 1964 |
> | 34 | Can name the current Secretary of State | 1978 |
> | 30 | Know that the term of U.S. House member is two years | 1978 |
> | 28 | Can name their state senator | 1967 |
> | 23 | Know which two nations are involved in SALT talks | 1979 |
>
> **Sources: New York Times,** 15 April 1986; Robert Erikson, Norman R. Lutbeg, and Kent L. Tedin, **American Public Opinion: Its Origins, Content, and Impact,** 2nd ed. (New York: Wiley, 1980), 19.

groups that typically have considerable resources—and this bias introduces major distortions into public debate. Unless political organizations reduce the costs of information for individual voters, they will be victimized by that bias.[12]

But if organization is enormously important, popular organization is largely absent in the U.S., again underscoring the exceptionalism of

American politics. In most West European nations, for example, the majority of wage and salary workers belong to unions, or are covered by union contracts. In Sweden, to take an extreme example, the unionization rate routinely runs in excess of 80 percent. In the U.S., by contrast, only 18 percent of employed wage and salary workers are organized, less than a quarter of the Swedish share.[13]

Outside such "secondary" institutions as unions, moreover, the peculiar fragmentation of U.S. politics is both reflected and advanced in the "primary" institutions of conventional politics. Many aspects of the political system might be used to support this claim—from the absence of a labor or socialist party noted earlier to the rules on campaign financing in the U.S. Here we will focus on just two important aspects of the conventional political system: political parties and electoral participation.

Parties

In modern states, political parties are the chief means of organizing politics, and ideally perform a variety of functions. Through the electoral process, they systematize the transfer of legitimate power by competing for control of the state. They also organize conflict *within* government, by defining the terms of debate, and organizing the process of issue-clarification and negotiation necessary to concerted action.

A third function that parties ideally perform is to articulate and clarify policy choices in ways that facilitate meaningful participation by wide numbers of ordinary citizens. This function is particularly important in a democratic system, and for that reason we concentrate on it here.

By taking positions on specific issues—tax reform, farm policy, military spending—and by fitting those positions into broader political programs and platforms, parties can help to simplify complex decisions. The effect of this is to lower the costs to voters of making such decisions, and thus relieve the information costs just noted. Consider, for example, the use of party "labels." Someone may not know much about the particular candidates for a particular office. But, ideally, knowing that Jones is a Republican and Smith is a Democrat should tell them something about the commitments of the candidates and how they will behave in office. Further, parties can reduce the costs of establishing political coalitions. For a civil rights group to go into coalition with a peace group, for example, the two have to sit down and work through the conditions under which they will act together. Such negotiation is often difficult, and always time consuming. By facilitating such negotiations, parties can encourage more effective participation by wider numbers of citizens.

As might be expected from the features of American politics discussed in Part 1, the degree to which American political parties serve to clarify issues and integrate diverse interests is limited. And this failure, in turn, further raises the costs of participation for ordinary people.

Just Two Parties

Perhaps the most obvious aspect of party competition in the U.S. is that there are only two parties seriously competing. Among capitalist democracies, this too is exceptional. In most such countries—England, France, Germany, and elsewhere—several parties are represented in the national legislature. It is not that Americans have never tried to form "third parties." Since the 1820s, indeed, there have been more than a thousand formed. But while third parties here have often been useful indicators of rising popular dissatisfaction with the two major parties, their role in American politics is distinctly limited. Only 12 of the more than a thousand third parties just cited, for example, ever gained 6 percent or more of the vote in an election for national office (see Table 3).

Two different factors help to explain the problems of third parties. First, since the 1840s national U.S. politics has universally adopted *single-member districts* as the basis for representation, and has rejected systems of *proportional representation*. In a single-member district system, as its name indicates, only one representative is elected in any election district. The winner of the election in that district gets the seat; the loser(s) get(s) nothing. In a single-member district system, for example, if Candidate A gets 60 percent of the vote, Candidate B gets 30 percent, and Candidate C (in case there is a third party in the district) gets 10 percent, only Candidate A goes to the legislature.

In a system of proportional representation, on the other hand, election districts commonly comprise the entire country, or large regions of it; candidates run together on different party slates; and the distribution of legislative seats conforms to the distribution of the vote. Assuming a large district with 100 representatives assigned to it, if Party A took 60 percent of the vote, it would get 60 of those seats; Party B, with 30 percent, would get 30; and Party C, with 10 percent, would get 10.

Single-member district systems tend to discourage the formation of third parties. Since the "winner takes all," a third party (like any other party) has to actually win, and not merely do well, for it to gain representation. Knowing this, and fearing that their efforts will be "wasted," potential supporters of such a party are commonly reluctant to offer their support.

A second set of barriers arises from the difficulties third parties have in even getting on the ballot—difficulties that the two dominant parties have done their best to erect. While the basic costs of electoral competition in the U.S. are very high, for would-be third parties—which must repeatedly justify their existence by meeting all sorts of cumbersome filing requirements, including signature showings that large numbers of voters want them on the ballot—the costs are higher still. As John Anderson, Eugene McCarthy, and other recent major independent candidates can attest, a major part of the costs of even getting started on a national third party challenge consists in struggling to meet these requirements.[14]

Table 3: Major Third Parties in American History

Party	Year of Maximum	Percentage of Vote	
Anti-Masonic	1832	7.8	Proto "Populist" movement against elitism and "privilege"
Free Soil	1848	10.1	Antislavery protest against both major parties
American	1856	21.5	Anti-Catholic southern fragment of the Whig party
Constitutional Union	1860	12.6	Southern fragment of the (now dead) Whig party
Southern Democrat	1860	18.1	Bolters from nomination of Stephen A. Douglas; proto-Confederate
Greenback	1878	12.9	Farmer (and some labor) groups opposed to currency deflation and resumption of **de facto** gold standard
Populist	1894	11.5	Opposition to industrial capitalism and continuing currency deflation
Socialist	1912	6.0	High-water mark of socialist movement in opposition to industrial capitalism
Progressive	1912	27.4	Bolters from nomination of William H. Taft (R); supporters of Theodore Roosevelt
Progressive	1924	16.6	Farmer-labor protest coalition against conservative business control of both parties
American Independent (George Wallace)	1968	13.5	Protest against civil-rights revolution, cosmopolitan cultural and political elites, etc.; very strong in South
Independent (John Anderson)	1980	6.6	Liberal Republicans and some "New Class" Democrats opposed to both Ronald Reagan and Jimmy Carter

Source: Walter Dean Burnham, **Democracy in the Making: American Government and Politics,** 2nd ed. (Englewood Cliffs, NJ: Prentice-Hall, 1986), 251.

Party Weakness and Failure

Given all the other constraints on popular organization, and especially given the failure of socialist and labor parties, the reduction of the electoral universe to two major parties encourages three important characteristics of conventional politics in the U.S.

First, as *organizations* the parties are relatively weak. Handling the incredibly diverse interests thrown up by a fragmented political system within only two organizations virtually requires that those organizations themselves be relatively weak, without strong top-down hierarchies of control. This organizational weakness is encouraged by many other aspects of the political system already noted. The separation of power between the executive and Congress, for example, means that governments in the United States do not need to command majority partisan support to function; as a consequence, less of a premium is placed on party discipline. In addition, the localistic character of politics means that such discipline would be that much harder to achieve, even if it were desired. As a result, parties in the U.S. are best thought of as intensely coalitional groupings, with different groups within the same party commonly enjoying only tenuous relations with one another. Within the New Deal Democratic coalition, for example, reactionary southern elites and the most progressive elements of the American labor movement both identified themselves as Democrats. But they had little in common beyond their party label. More recently, the existence of "boll weevil" Democrats who voted with the Reagan administration, and "gypsy moth" Republicans who voted against it, has underscored the diversity of coalitions within both parties.

A second feature of American parties flows naturally from the first. Because they are organizationally weak, the parties do not commonly articulate clear policy choices. Indeed, parties in the U.S. are not really policy organizations, intent upon the presentation of coherent programs for action, but *constituency organizations*, intent upon providing benefits and services for the coalitions that comprise them. The politics of fragmentation is reflected in the absence of a commitment to organize debate along sharp partisan lines, and in the difficulties of organizing debate on issues of broad national concern, which cut across diverse and competing coalitions.

A third feature of American parties, also specifically encouraged by the existence of only two parties, is that the positions the parties do take are commonly *very close together*, with one party just a shade to the left, or the right, of the other. Since the two major parties are "the only ballgames in town," and barriers to third parties are so high, such positioning is commonly a rational strategy for maximizing support. But just as commonly it serves to further constrain the range of political debate, and confuse the consideration of issues.

These three familiar features of American political parties—their lack of discipline, their non-programmatic constituency focus, and the narrow range of alternatives they present—all serve to undermine the democratizing

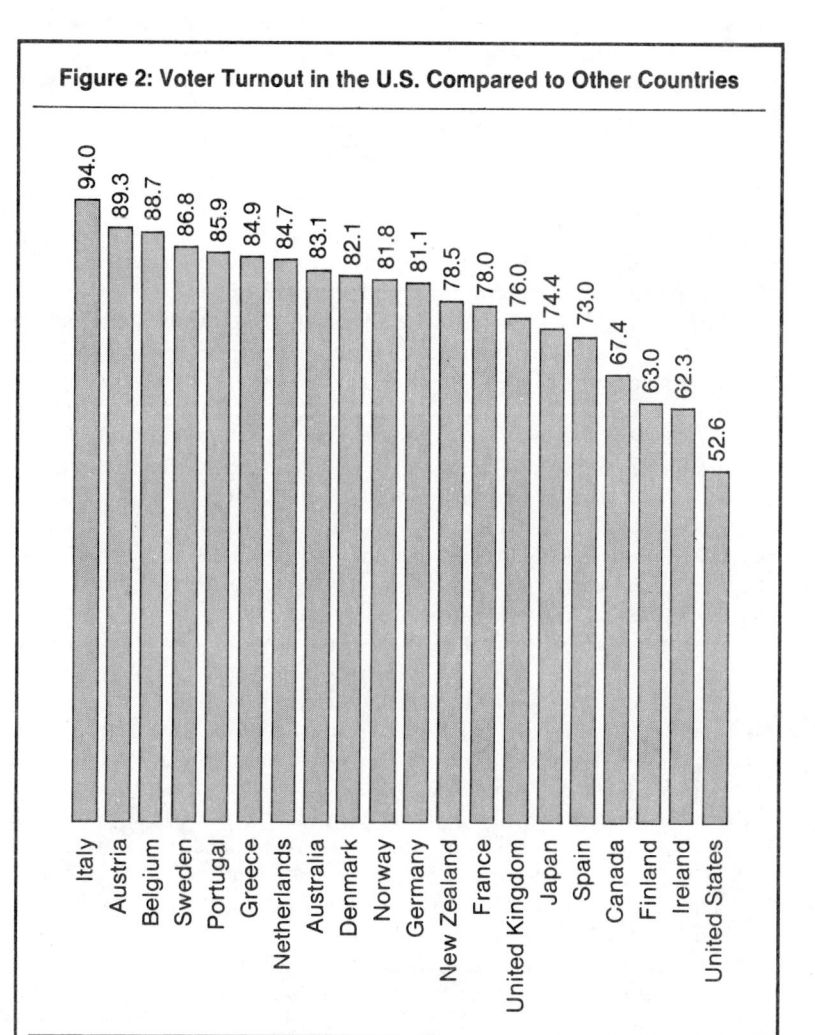

Figure 2: Voter Turnout in the U.S. Compared to Other Countries

Country	Turnout
Italy	94.0
Austria	89.3
Belgium	88.7
Sweden	86.8
Portugal	85.9
Greece	84.9
Netherlands	84.7
Australia	83.1
Denmark	82.1
Norway	81.8
Germany	81.1
New Zealand	78.5
France	78.0
United Kingdom	76.0
Japan	74.4
Spain	73.0
Canada	67.4
Finland	63.0
Ireland	62.3
United States	52.6

Source: David Glass, Peverill Squire, and Raymond Wolfinger, "Voter Turnout: an International Comparison," **Public Opinion** 7 (December-January 1984): 50. The data reflect the most recent national election in each country, as of 1981. Note that the denominator used here in deriving the participation rate is the voting age population (VAP). In the U.S. case, this includes aliens and convicted felons, who cannot vote, while excluding citizens living abroad, who can. Because the VAP is bigger than the eligible electorate, the denominator used in the text, it yields a slightly lower estimate of participation.

function of parties noted above. Without strong, programmatic, and ideologically competitive parties, it is extremely difficult for citizens of average means to overcome the various costs of political action. In the U.S. the existing parties do very little to relieve this problem. Indeed, by continually reproducing the politics of fragmentation, they often make it worse.

Voting

The peculiarities of the American political system extend to the behavior of voters, and are highlighted by the basic characteristics of electoral participation. Again, three points are critical.

The first is that relatively few people in the U.S. vote. In 1984, only 55 percent of the eligible electorate cast ballots for President. Some 76 million eligible Americans—21 million more than voted for Ronald Reagan—abstained. Voting in Congressional races is even lower. In "off-year" (that is, non-presidential election year) Congressional races, less than 40 percent of the eligible electorate votes. In comparative terms, these figures are staggering. In Western Europe, for example, participation rates typically run 20-30 points higher (see Figure 2). In his 1984 landslide reelection, for example, President Reagan claimed a smaller share of the eligible American electorate than Valery Giscard d'Estaing claimed of the eligible French electorate when he *lost* to Francois Mitterand in 1981.[15]

Second, participation in the U.S. is "class-skewed." The wealthy vote at much higher rates than the poor, and the level of participation in between moves consistently with social and economic position. In the 1980 election, for example, an estimated 70 percent of Americans with annual incomes in excess of $25,000 voted, while only 25 percent of those with annual incomes of less than $10,000 did; 81 percent of those with college degrees cast ballots, while just 51 percent of those with only a grammar school education did. This too contrasts markedly with other nations, which do not feature such wide variation in participation between classes. One study, for example, found that in Sweden the "propertied middle class" voted at a 90 percent rate, while in the U.S. the same class voted at a 77 percent rate; for the "non-propertied middle class" the participation rates were 90 percent and 70 percent, respectively; for craftsmen and foremen, 93 and 58 percent; for workers, 87 and 47 percent. Thus the participation rate diffference of 13 percentage points at the upper income level widened to 40 points near the bottom.[16]

The third essential point about electoral participation in the U.S. is that it was not always so low or so skewed. In fact, in terms of electoral participation the U.S. was far more democratic—both on its own terms, and in comparison to Europe—in the 19th century than it is today. The absence of traditionalist social forces (church and aristocracy) and the widespread dispersion of land-ownership permitted the early extension of suffrage to virtually all of the white male population. Universal white male suffrage was virtually complete by 1830, in a "constitutional revolution" that enjoyed very broad elite, as well as mass support.

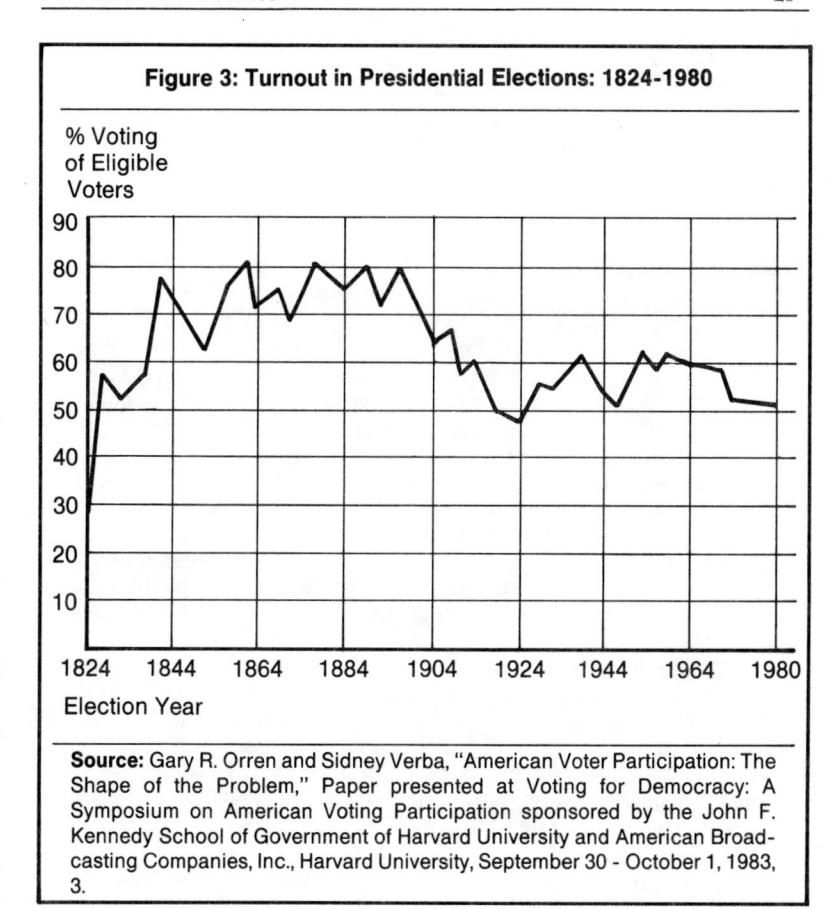

Figure 3: Turnout in Presidential Elections: 1824-1980

Source: Gary R. Orren and Sidney Verba, "American Voter Participation: The Shape of the Problem," Paper presented at Voting for Democracy: A Symposium on American Voting Participation sponsored by the John F. Kennedy School of Government of Harvard University and American Broadcasting Companies, Inc., Harvard University, September 30 - October 1, 1983, 3.

For much of the 19th century the U.S. enjoyed levels of voter participation comparable to those Western Europe enjoys today, with national rates of participation running in the 70-80 percent range (see Figure 3). Participation then dropped sharply after the 1890s. Here again America presents an exceptional case. In contrast to all other countries, and in direct conflict with the general rule that increasing living standards and education will lead to increasing turnout, the American voter "appeared," and then "disappeared."[17]

Part of the explanation for this puzzle, surely, was the imposition of a variety of restrictions on voting following the defeat of the Populists in the 1890s. The next two decades saw the widespread imposition of personal periodic registration and literacy tests as a requirement for voting, the abolition of alien voting, and, especially in the South, the use of a variety of other exclusionary practices, including poll taxes requiring payment to vote,

**Box 4:
Realignment, Dealignment,
and the Importance of Parties**

The idea of a "party system," such as the System of 1896 or the New Deal system, is closely associated with the idea of "realignment," a term used to describe massive shifts in public policy. Such realignments have occurred periodically in American politics. Most observers agree, for example, that the Jacksonian revolution, the Civil War, the 1890s, and the New Deal all marked periods of major policy change. Many, ourselves included, argue that another such major change in public policy is occurring now in Washington.

Just what produces policy changes of this magnitude, however, is a matter of continuing dispute. According to the theory of "critical elections," realignments are caused by massive shifts among groups of voters. In short, a realignment of voters produces a realignment of policy. But this theory has been cast in doubt by difficulties in identifying periods of policy realignment with periods of voter realignment.

Whatever the resolution of disputes about the source of previous realignments, however, it is generally conceded that the present period of policy change has **not** been associated with massive changes in the electorate. Despite major Republican victories at the Presidential level in 1980 and 1984, Congressional and state offices remain largely in Democratic hands. Indeed, over the 1980-84 period, Democrats actually **gained** seats in Congress, something that would not be expected if a Republican realignment was underway.

Some observers refer to this result as a "split-level realignment," referring to the fact that Congressional and Presidential elections do not seem to move together. But however the recent results are to be described, they seem to be an instance of a more general phenomenon, known as "dealignment," observed in recent years. Broadly speaking, dealignment refers to the decline of political parties as the most important organizers of political debate and choice among voters, and the consequent decline in partisan voting. One measure of this phenomenon is the percentage of voters reporting having "split" their ballots between the two major parties. While different surveys generate different numbers on this question, all report a substantial increase in split-ticket voting over the past generation.

Another way to gauge the scope of the phenomenon is to look at the percentage of Congressional districts choosing a Presidential candidate from one party, and a Representative from another. This too has trended sharply upward over the past generation. In 1952, for example, only 19.3 percent of Congressional districts split their vote in this way; in 1984, 43.7 did.

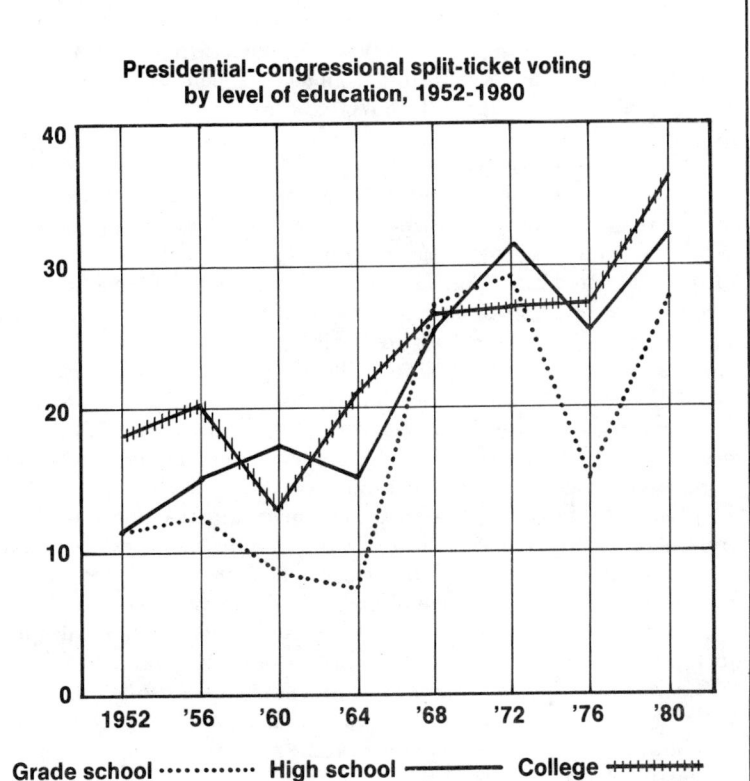

Presidential-congressional split-ticket voting by level of education, 1952-1980

Grade school ············ High school ——— College ++++++++

Finally, as the importance of party affiliation declines, one would also expect that the natural advantages of incumbency would weigh more heavily in determining Congressional outcomes, and the number of close Congressional elections would decline. Here the 1984 data are particularly striking. Of the 435 seats in the House, 408 (a record) were contested by incumbents, and only 16 of those incumbents (another record) lost. Some 75 percent of all House races (another record) were won by 60 percent or more of the vote.

Sources: Martin P. Wattenberg, **The Decline of American Political Parties 1952-1980** (Cambridge, MA: Harvard University Press, 1984), 117; John A. Ferejohn and Morris P. Fiorina, "Incumbency and Realignment in Congressional Elections," in **The New Direction in American Politics,** ed. John E. Chubb and Paul E. Peterson (Washington, DC: Brookings Institution, 1985), 100; Burnham, "The 1984 Election," 239-40.

"grandfather" clauses excluding the grandchildren of slaves from the suffrage, and use of the "white primary" (in which only white people could vote) to manage candidate selection in the totally Democratic dominated region. By the beginning of World War I, national turnout declined about a quarter from its 1896 level, falling from 80 to 62 percent. The story of the South, as always, was especially dramatic. Turnout there tumbled to as low as 19 percent by 1924.

Such barriers, however, are only part of the story. With the important exception of the uniquely American requirement of personal registration, most have since been struck down, but turnout has not substantially revived. While the New Deal saw a partial remobilization of the electorate, voter turnout stagnated in the postwar period. And since 1960, even as substantial progress was being made in removing barriers to the free exercise of the suffrage, some 20 million registered voters have dropped out of the active voting pool, bringing participation to its present dismal level. What is going on here, we suspect, has to do less with the procedures of American politics than with its substance. To develop this point, however, requires shifting from a broad characterization of the framework of American politics to a discussion of the evolution of that framework.

The 1890s saw a "realignment" in American party politics—a major shift in public policy, and in the structure of competition between the major parties. The "System of 1896," so called because of the pivotal election in that year, ushered in a long period of Republican dominance in national policy, and a distinctive set of policies—including high tariffs and the eradication of such popular organizations as the Populists—directed to consolidating the U.S. as a major industrial power. It would not be until the New Deal of the 1930s that another realignment came, and, distinctively, that popular organizations of workers in the U.S. came to wield significant power in national electoral politics.

The System of 1896, however, signified more than the move from one party system to another. It also coincided with the final transit from the "liberal capitalism" that marked the 19th century to the "organized" capitalism characteristic of the modern period. The latter is associated with greater degrees of industrial concentration, the rise of the modern corporation, and the full emergence of national and subsequently multinational firms and markets. It is also associated with the transformation of the U.S. from a predominantly agrarian society to a fully industrial one, with the vast bulk of workers dependent on markets for wage labor.

What defines organized capitalism as a *political* phenomenon, however, is increased direct state involvement in the organization of economic life. The state came to play a more affirmative role in reordering private markets, promoting business enterprise, and regulating wage labor. This expanded state role was seen as necessary to managing the conflicts and demands of the new economic order. But taking on these new tasks, in turn, required a major reorganization and enhancement of the capacities of the state itself. In a word, the American state had to become stronger.

Such a strengthening could have been achieved by breaking down some of the barriers to popular democratic action in the U.S., and this path was promoted by the various populist movements of the time. Higher levels of political organization could have reduced the costs of making complex decisions, facilitated bargaining among diverse interests, and thus cleared the channels of political authority from the people to the government. Once the people were involved in decision making, the pattern of state action could be expected to change. Still, such a democratization could have given the state both broad capacities to act, and popular support in doing so.

But this was not the route taken. Instead, the major powers in American society chose to "simplify" decisions by reducing democracy, and limiting the range of active participants in the formulation of public policy. This reduction was achieved in two ways. First, as already noted, large numbers of the active electorate, predominantly the poorer elements in the electorate, were driven from the scene. This directly "simplified" the consideration of issues of public policy, since it excluded those elements of the population most interested in using the state to redress material inequalities. Over time, this exclusion became self-enforcing. Since public policy did not aim to address the concerns of the poorest and most dependent parts of the population, there was little incentive for them to reenter the system even after formal participation barriers were broken down. Second, and more subtly, the center of gravity of policy formation within government shifted. Many of the new tasks of the state were assumed by the executive branch, whose administrative bureaucracy was insulated from direct electoral pressures. For ordinary Americans, who had enjoyed only the most imperfect access to legislative arenas to begin with, influencing this executive bureaucracy was virtually impossible.

As a general matter, the likelihood of an individual or group participating in electoral politics depends directly on the costs of that participation, and on the expectation of benefits. After the 1890s, the difficulties of electoral participation increased dramatically for ordinary Americans. And the benefits of participation seemed, accurately, to be increasingly remote. With popular organizations in disarray, national politics largely inattentive to the needs of the poorer and more dependent classes, and public policy increasingly detached from electoral arenas altogether, it is no wonder that political participation declined sharply at the turn of the century, or that it has resumed that decline over the past two decades.

The exception to all this, of course, is the New Deal—a time when the content of public policy, and the organizations of popular politics, briefly promised to reverse the demobilization of the American electorate. It is time now to consider that exception, and the profound consequences, which extend well beyond participation rates, of the recent collapse of the New Deal system. This brings us to the *content* of recent American politics, which imposes a third set of constraints on democratic action.

3. Right Turn: American Politics in the 1980s

Great changes in American politics typically emerge out of economic crises. Economic crises jolt existing elite coalitions, and often create mass pressures on those coalitions from below. This was true of the System of 1896, and it was certainly true of the New Deal. During the Great Depression, personal income plummeted, the number of business failures soared, and the unemployment rate rose as high as 25 percent. The depression was worldwide, and in some countries (such as Germany) the pressures it induced shattered all pretense to democracy. Deepening conflicts among the world's great economies led to massive programs of protectionism, as different nations struggled to defend themselves against the disruptions of international competition. Eventually, of course, World War II resulted from the conflicts engendered by these reorganizations of "national purpose."

In the U.S., as millions of workers took to the streets, and socialist and communist organizations made serious bids for the loyalties of significant numbers of Americans, popular protest and upheaval surged forward. But basic electoral institutions in the U.S. remained intact. Instead of a New Order, Americans got a New Deal—a set of programs and policies, centrally identifed with the Democratic Party, which had broad appeal to both critical emergent sectors of the business community and the mass public.[18]

The New Deal had both a domestic and international component. At home, it stood for the first major moves toward social welfare programs (Social Security, unemployment insurance, massive public works projects) and the protection of workers' rights to organize themselves into unions. It sharply increased the direct regulation and control of business (in addition to business promotion). And it dedicated the government to curbing the disastrous swings of business cycles—the booms and busts of the unregulated economy—through macroeconomic policy.

Abroad, the initiatives Roosevelt made in the 1930s, which were consolidated in the immediate postwar period, committed the U.S. to the promotion of free trade and expanding "multilateralism," or cooperation among the major capitalist powers in the pursuit of this goal. Leading portions of U.S. business were willing to support such a policy, which contrasted pointedly with the high-tariff regime that had preceded it, because U.S. industry was now the most competitive in the world.[19]

Because it bears so heavily on efforts to change foreign policy, it is worth emphasizing that the postwar consolidation of the New Deal's international component also saw the rise of the "national security state"—a massive bureaucracy, centered on the President, that took charge of the conduct of U.S. foreign policy.

In some measure, this executive-centered leadership of foreign policy was continuous with previous history. The Constitution grants the President special powers in the conduct of foreign policy, and the general displacement of policy decisions out of legislative arenas and into executive/administrative ones was, as noted earlier, part and parcel of the transition to "modern" politics signalled by the System of 1896.

But the postwar period saw a qualitative rise in the importance of the military and foreign policy role of the U.S. As emphasized in the earlier pamphlet in this series, *Inequity and Intervention,* it was during the immediate postwar period that the U.S. assumed leadership of the "free world," and reigned as dominant power within a reordered capitalist system. Peacetime military spending soared, and came to play a central role in the domestic economy, as the U.S. committed itself to maintaining a global military presence. Within the vastly expanded federal bureaucracy, the Department of Defense dominated, claiming more than half the Federal budget throughout the 1950s, and more employees than all other executive departments combined. And within the policy making process, an "Imperial Presidency" emerged, with the Chief Executive and Commander in Chief enjoying unprecedented control over foreign and military commitments. Precisely at the moment that the U.S. international role became more important, it became significantly less accountable to democratic institutions (see Table 4 and Box 5). This point informs the discussion, in Part 4 below, about changing the course of present U.S. policies in Central America.

The Decline of Labor

From the perspective of popular politics, the New Deal marked a watershed in American history. It was the first time that the government explicitly committed itself—through legislation like the Wagner Act, protecting the formation of unions; the Fair Labor Standards Act, setting national minimum wages and maximum hours; and the Social Security Act, establishing a mechanism to provide workers income after retirement—to promoting the welfare of workers as well as business. More immediately, as

Table 4: Who Shapes U.S. Foreign Policy?

"How important a role do you think the following currently play in determining the foreign policy of the United States—a very important role, a somewhat important role, or hardly an important role at all?"

Percent "Very Important"

	Public 1982	Leaders 1982
The President	70	91
Secretary of State	64	83
State Department	47	38
Congress	46	34
National Security Adviser	35	46
American Business	35	22
The Military	40	36
United Nations	29	2
The CIA	28	20
Public Opinion	23	15
Labor Unions	17	3

Source: John E. Reilly, ed., **American Public Opinion and U.S. Foreign Policy 1983** (Chicago: Chicago Council on Foreign Relations, 1983), 33.

militant workers enforced the Wagner Act's protections through direct action of their own, unionization soared. Workers *organized* themselves, and as organized blocs were able, really for the first time in American history, to exert some measure of ongoing influence on the workings of national politics. Formally non-partisan, the major unions forged a working alliance with the Democratic Party, and sought through that party to influence the course of national public policy.

For a brief time, the organization of working people held out the promise of reversing some of the fragmenting tendencies of American politics, and the special difficulties that system creates for popular collective action. With unions on the rise, it was possible to imagine broader forms of collective association extending out from them, and a deeper democratization of American politics from below. This promise, however, was never redeemed. And the fact that it was not bears closer examination here, for it highlights the difficulties, even under the best of circumstances, of popular politics in the U.S.

As a general matter, it is important to recognize the fragility of labor's initial gains, particularly as those gains relied upon benevolent state action.

> **Box 5: The Growing Presidential Role in Foreign Policy**
>
> The Constitution gives the President the power to make treaties "by and with the advice and consent of the Senate," and requires a two-thirds vote for treaty approval. Executive agreements, by contrast, do not require Senate approval. The increasing proportion of executive agreements as a share of international agreements shown below thus provides one indicator of the growing importance of the President in foreign policy after World War II.
>
> | Period | Treaties | Executive Agreements | Total | Executive Agreements as % of Total |
> |---|---|---|---|---|
> | 1789-1839 | 60 | 27 | 87 | 31% |
> | 1839-1889 | 215 | 238 | 453 | 53% |
> | 1889-1939 | 524 | 917 | 1,141 | 64% |
> | 1940-1973 | 364 | 6,395 | 6,759 | 95% |
> | 1974-1979 | 102 | 2,233 | 2,335 | 96% |
> | 1980-1982 | 55 | 1,063 | 1,118 | 95% |
>
> **Source:** Congressional Research Service, Library of Congress.

Even at the high point of its influence, labor was always a distinctly junior partner in the New Deal coalition, and it soon became clear that the terms of its incorporation in the Democratic Party served to prolong the exceptionalism of the U.S. case. As early as 1947, with the passage of the Taft-Hartley Act and its many restrictions on union activities, national politics turned away from the promotion of unionization. And almost immediately thereafter, the unionized percentage of the workforce, which had reached a postwar high of about 39 percent of private non-agricultural employment, commenced the long decline that continues to this day (see Figure 4).

Labor's strength *within* the Democratic party also declined in obvious ways. Despite routine promises from party leaders, for example, labor was never able to improve the conditions of its own organization through the party's action. Even during the very heavily Democratic Congresses of the mid-1960s it was unable to compel a reform of Taft-Hartley's infamous section 14(b), which discourages unionization by giving state legislatures the right to pass "right to work" laws restricting union control over job sites. And throughout the 1970s organized labor was unable to secure any of the more modest reforms it sought in the administration of labor law. Indeed, in every major legislative battle that pitted the interests of unions against other major interests in the Democratic party during the post-New Deal era, labor lost.

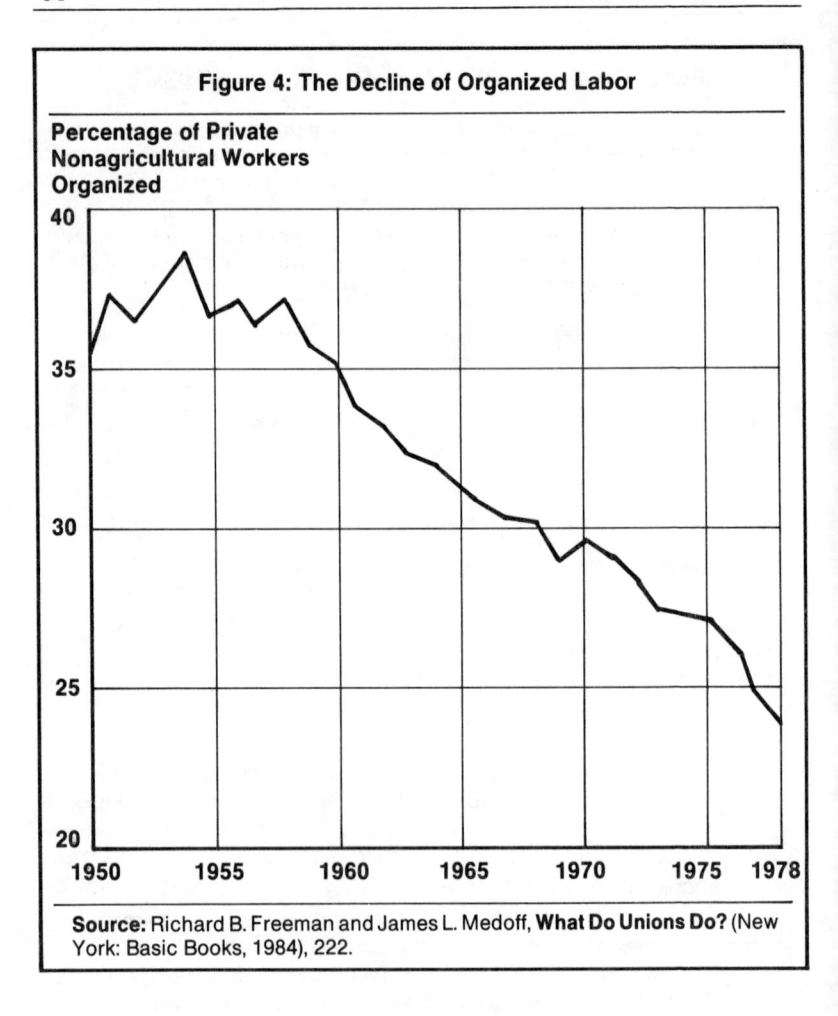

Figure 4: The Decline of Organized Labor

Percentage of Private Nonagricultural Workers Organized

[Line graph showing decline from approximately 38% in 1950 to approximately 24% in 1978, with the x-axis marking years 1950, 1955, 1960, 1965, 1970, 1975, 1978 and the y-axis marking 20, 25, 30, 35, 40.]

Source: Richard B. Freeman and James L. Medoff, **What Do Unions Do?** (New York: Basic Books, 1984), 222.

Labor's decline in power has many sources. Considered at the level of national politics, however, its most obvious problem was that it had only regional power—primarily along the coasts, and the Northeast and Midwest. In a political system as heterogeneous as the U.S., logrolling and the trading of favors across differently situated regional interests comprise the basis of most legislative action. In many parts of the country, however, and in particular in the South, labor had very little with which to deal.

But if the failure to organize the South was a central political failure of organized labor, that failure was itself symptomatic of the broad features of U.S. politics already described. The South was the least developed region of the country; thus the potential for organizing, and the direct payoffs to unions of doing it, were less than in other portions of the country.

Organizing in the South would also require confrontation with the peculiar institutions of southern politics, and the oppression of black people upon which they relied; but this was something that overwhelmingly white-led unions were not prepared to do (particularly after they had purged their more radical members). Nor was the Democratic Party prepared to act aggressively for labor in that region. For even as the party promoted social welfare legislation, it relied on the support of reactionary southern elites, who staunchly opposed the unionization of their local workforces. Content with its status as junior partner, labor was never itself willing to seriously contest that issue.

More generally, and especially after the increased barriers to unionization created by Taft-Hartley, the focus of the labor movement shifted from the mobilization of broad sectors of the population to the protection of gains made by its own members. Locked into a system of regulation that encouraged a focus on short term gains, it commonly pursued those gains to the exclusion of broader issues of social justice.

This point should not be overstated. In general, labor remained the most consistently progressive organized element in American society; but there were severe limits to its agenda, and even more severe ones on the support it would extend to other struggles. These limits became pointedly evident during the 1960s. Despite support for most of the landmark civil rights legislation of that period, labor's relations with the civil rights movement were always strained, and often openly antagonistic; its relations with the women's movement were even worse; and it was a tireless booster of U.S. intervention abroad, which divided it from the huge movement opposed to the U.S. invasion of Vietnam. The most obvious sources of support for a further democratization of American society—the civil rights movement, the antiwar movement, and the women's movement—were either only grudgingly supported, or openly attacked, by the only arguably popular organization with the resources necessary for political action.

Even as it turned aside such potential allies, however, and even as the organized percentage of the workforce continued to slide, organized labor remained serene about its own prospects. Wages of union members rose with the great boom of the 1960s; from the perspective of short term gains, things were going well. Only a few years later, however, the scope of its organizational failures, and those of the movements it declined to aid, would become shockingly apparent.

The Collapse of the New Deal System

If the Great Depression of the 1930s ushered in a period of national dominance for the Democratic Party, what finally fractured the New Deal, and the Democrats with it, was the more subtle economic crisis that gripped the American economy in the 1970s. Particularly after the great recession of 1973-75, it became clear that the structure of the world economy, and America's place within it, had changed drastically.[20]

At home, the long generation of growth that had brought rising living standards for millions of Americans abruptly slowed. Profits had already peaked in 1965, and continued to decline; investment fell off sharply; productivity fell; annual growth in real GNP tumbled from just over 4 percent over the 1960-73 period to just over 2 percent for the rest of the 1970s. Wages skidded downward, and median family income, which had doubled over the postwar generation, dramatically declined.

Even more significant for American politics was the changed international picture. As already noted, a vital source of support for New Deal commitments was the highly competitive position of leading sections of U.S. business. By the 1970s, however, the competitiveness of U.S. industry had come under sharp challenge. In 1971, for the first time since the 1890s, the U.S. imported more than it exported. Import penetration increased throughout the 1970s, and world market shares of U.S. businesses, even in advanced industrial sectors, shrank. More significant still, as it was losing out in international competition, U.S. business was also becoming increasingly *integrated* into the world economy (see Table 5).

Particularly important was the United States' increased interest in, and connection to, the Third World, which was then growing at rates roughly double those sustained among the advanced industrial states. The great rise in oil prices that marked the emergence of OPEC served to heighten this involvement in various ways. OPEC nations emerged as major markets for U.S. goods and services. And the excess dollars they reaped from windfall oil price increases were commonly deposited in U.S. banks, which promptly loaned them back out to other Third World countries in the form of debt.

These developments had two related effects on the American business community.

First, increasing competitive pressures and sagging profit margins made virtually all sections of that community much more sensitive to costs, anxious to cut those that could be moderated through the political system, and willing to mobilize to ensure a favorable political response. Although U.S. labor costs were already falling in comparative terms, for example, they became an object of wide business attack. Groups like the National Association of Manufacturers promoted the virtues of a "union-free environment," and at the National Labor Relations Board (the federal agency charged with enforcing the nation's basic labor law) findings of illegal "unfair labor practices" by employers skyrocketed. While the costs of regulation in the U.S. were also relatively low in comparative terms, business organizations—including a revived Chamber of Commerce, the new Business Roundtable, and a host of private foundations—mobilized to cut back on the "regulatory burden" imposed by government. While the level of welfare spending in the U.S. was already very low in comparative terms, widespread efforts—reflected in the efforts of such business supported "think tanks" as the Heritage Foundation and the American Enterprise Institute— soon got underway to chop social spending and return to the "free" labor

Table 5: The Internationalization of the U.S. Economy			
	1960	1970	1980
Exports as % of GNP	4.0	4.3	8.2
Imports as % of GNP	3.0	4.0	9.2
Export of Manufacturers as % Manufactured Goods GDP	8.8	11.6	24.3
Import of Manufacturers as % of Manufactured Goods GDP	4.8	10.3	21.3
U.S. Foreign Investment Abroad	$30.4b	$75.6b	$215.5b
Profit on Investment Abroad as % total Corporate profits	12.2	21.8	23.0
Direct Foreign Investment in U.S.	—	$13.2b	$68.4b
Foreign Assets U.S. Banks as % Total Assets U.S. Banks	1.5	12.2	26.0

Source: James M. Cypher, "Monetarism, Militarism and Markets: Reagan's Response to the Structural Crisis," **MERIP Reports** 14 (November-December 1984): 10.

market. Last but hardly least, while effective corporate tax rates were already falling dramatically, much of business—gathering in groups like the American Council on Capital Formation, or later, the so-called Carlton Group—mobilized to cut back on business tax costs.

Second, growing U.S. involvement in the Third World, especially during a period of increasing competition with other powers, underscored for many within the business community the desirability of enhancing U.S. capacities to project force abroad. This development destructively interacted with the waning of elite commitments to *detente,* which had not brought the benefits to the U.S. that many of its original proponents had expected. As a consequence, pressure mounted—reflected in the revival of many Cold War groups, and the formation of the elite Committee on the Present Danger—for a major modernization and enhancement of U.S. military capabilities.

U.S. business thus reacted to the economic pressures it encountered in predictable ways. Unable, because of its own divisions, to mount a concerted response to international competition and domestic restructuring, it sought to force the costs of restructuring onto workers. And unwilling to engage in the mammoth job of negotiating a fairer distribution of international power, it sought to increase its ability to impose its will on other nations.

This response had different effects on the Democratic and Republican parties. For the Democrats, it created profound, and finally unbearable tensions between the needs of the party's mass base and the demands of its elite business constituency. Simultaneous demands for tax reductions and a major military buildup inevitably squeezed social programs, on which the Democrats relied to provide themselves with a mass base. At the same time, however weakened that base was, organized portions of it provided some resistance to implementing a purely business oriented program. Public sector unions resisted cutbacks in educational spending and urban aid programs; social worker associations resisted further reductions in income maintenance programs; civil rights groups resisted cutbacks in minority hiring and employment training programs; elderly groups resisted further hikes in Medicaid deductibles; and the AFL-CIO, whatever its deficiencies, resisted further regressive revisions of the tax system. These sorts of tensions within Democratic ranks were highlighted by the presidency of Jimmy Carter, who tried to satisfy both elite and mass elements in the Democratic coalition, but wound up pleasing neither.

For the Republicans, on the other hand, who were unencumbered by a mass base, the shift to the right within the business community presented an enormous opportunity. Republicans were quite willing to serve as a vehicle for business aspirations, and to promote a broad program of attacks on workers, deregulation, cutbacks in social spending, business tax cuts, a military buildup, and a more assertive U.S. presence abroad. Especially in the late 1970s, many of the old business supporters of the Democrats abandoned the party, and threw their support to the GOP. Wealthy Americans swelled the Republican war chest (see Figure 5). And in 1980, the right turn was confirmed with the election of Ronald Reagan.

The New Party System

The years since Reagan's election to the presidency have seen enormous changes in American public policy. It is true that many of these changes had precedents in the last two years of the Carter administration. It is true too that some of the more extreme suggestions of the administration have been limited by opposition. Still, the policy initiatives of the past several years represent a striking departure from the basic principles that characterized the New Deal party system, and that were long embraced by Democrats and Republicans alike during that system's dominance. The administration has made significant cuts in social spending, particularly in low income programs, and made plain its desire for far deeper cuts; achieved a massive, and massively regressive, revision of the Federal tax system in 1981; dramatically scaled back the enforcement of regulations that posed any significant limits to business power; virtually abandoned the protection and promotion of minority and women's rights; openly attacked an already feeble labor movement; removed Federal supports from all manner of community organizations and advocacy groups; and, of course, at a time when military spending directly threatens social programs, sponsored the largest sustained peacetime military buildup in U.S. history. This may not

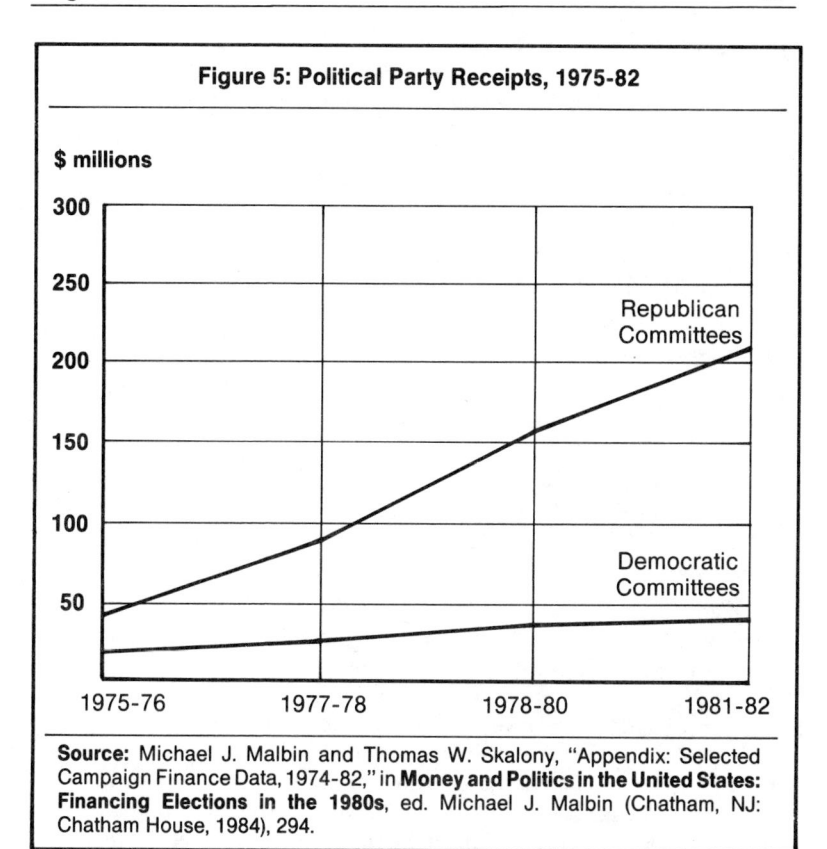

> **Figure 5: Political Party Receipts, 1975-82**
>
> [Line graph showing $ millions on y-axis (0-300) and years on x-axis (1975-76, 1977-78, 1978-80, 1981-82). Republican Committees line rises from ~45 to ~205. Democratic Committees line rises from ~20 to ~40.]
>
> **Source:** Michael J. Malbin and Thomas W. Skalony, "Appendix: Selected Campaign Finance Data, 1974-82," in **Money and Politics in the United States: Financing Elections in the 1980s**, ed. Michael J. Malbin (Chatham, NJ: Chatham House, 1984), 294.

comprise a coherent response to the problems of international competition and domestic economic decay. But it does consolidate a basic shift to the right in the center of gravity of the American political universe.

The existence of this shift is underscored by the fact that "Reaganism" is a joint product of Republicans and Democrats. Despite important continuing differences between the parties, the Democrats have bought into large elements of this program. The Democratic House, and many Democratic members of the Republican controlled Senate, endorsed the major tax and social spending initiatives of the administration and were strong supporters of Reagan's huge first-term military buildup (See Table 6). The Democrats also provided broad support for the Gramm-Rudman-Hollings bill that seeks permanent reductions in the scope of Federal activity. No "respectable" Democrat now proposes new domestic policy initiatives, or even increased support for old ones. And despite select criticisms and differences in emphasis, the Democrats have broadly endorsed the more

Table 6: Presidential Requests and Congressional Appropriations for the Military Budget, Fiscal Years 1980-85

Total obligational authority — Billions of dollars

Item	1980	1981	1982	1983	1984	1985
Presidential request	135.5	158.7	222.2a	258.0	274.1	305.7
Congressional appropriation	141.5	175.3	210.4	238.7	258.2	285.3
Change in amount	+6.0	+16.6	-11.8	-19.3	-15.9	-20.4
Change as percent of request	+4.4	+10.5	-5.3	-7.5	-5.8	-6.7

a. The original Carter request was for $196.4 billion. Reagan proposed adding $25.8 billion to this amount.

Source: William W. Kaufmann, **A Reasonable Defense** (Washington, DC: Brookings Institution, 1986), 25.

aggressive international policies pursued by the Reagan team. If the New Deal inaugurated a center-left party system, the past few years have seen the emergence of center-right one. The "terms of debate" in American politics have shifted.

It bears emphasis, as we implied at the very outset of this discussion, that what drove this process had almost nothing to do with changes in American public opinion. There is no evidence in opinion surveys that the public endorses social welfare cuts of the sort that have been put through in the past several years, or regressive tax changes, or rollbacks in environmental or health and safety legislation enforcement, or the abandonment of minority and women's rights, or a military buildup on the scale that has been achieved, or increased U.S. intervention abroad.[21]

Rather, as the preceding discussion implied, the shift to the right was precipitated by a realignment of American business elites in the face of a changing international environment. Such figures comprise the most powerful forces in both parties, and even as they compete among themselves, they are staunchly opposed to a broad reversal of present policies. Since no one would contest this judgment for the Republican party, we confine ourselves here to looking more closely at recent Democratic behavior.

The Democrats

What was the Democratic response to Ronald Reagan? As just argued, at the level of national policy, party representatives bought into substantial portions of the Reagan program. Even as they did so, however, they sought to position themselves as a more effective vehicle for presenting an alternative to Reagan that would still command substantial support within the business community. Doing so required both organizational and ideological changes in the party.

On the organizational side, the Democratic National Committee (DNC), under the leadership of lawyer-banker Charles Manatt, was a focus for various efforts to consolidate the party's internal operations. In straitened financial circumstances following the 1980 election, the DNC and Manatt tried to restrengthen the party's ties with business through efforts like the Democratic Business Council (DBC). This invited business members (at a cost of annual membership of $10,000 from individuals, or $15,000 from the individual's firm) to participate in various task force discussions to develop new party policies, and helped reestablish a working relationship with important funders. Manatt and other party leaders also actively sought out wealthy individuals to run for party office. The proliferation of such candidates, of course, would work directly to relieve strains on party finances, while also working to further solidify a more conservative Democratic leadership.

A correlate of these fundraising efforts were those of the Democratic Congressional Campaign Committee (DCCC), headed up by business-oriented California Congressman Tony Coelho. The DCCC also cultivated ties with corporate PACs and wealthy individual contributors, and emerged as an independent presence in the calculations of Democratic representatives. Anxious to receive the money of the labor movement, the DNC and the AFL-CIO leadership, most prominently Federation president Lane Kirkland, also worked out a deal to accord labor a more formal representation within the party's organizational structure.

The DNC, labor representatives, and other party elites also made major reforms in the internal rules on the nomination of candidates for national office. These rules changes rolled back most of the reforms of the early 1970s; they aimed, quite successfully as it turned out in the 1984 nomination process, at increasing the control of party leaders over the rank and file.

Particularly as the Reagan recession deepened in 1982, these various efforts began, literally, to pay off. As profits dropped and interest rates soared, many business figures grew distressed at the course of the "Reagan revolution." In addition to the obvious basic problems in economic performance, some that were oriented toward European markets were concerned about the administration's "hard line" on U.S.-European relations and its bullying of NATO allies; others, that were dependent upon government domestic programs for their own profits, thought the cutbacks had gone too far, or were not properly targeted; many, particularly within the financial sector, were alarmed at the apparently uncontrollable growth of the federal deficit; still others were alarmed at the staggering sums the administration was committing to "defense," or, in the case of numerous military contractors, critical of what the money was being spent for; and many firms, cracking under competitive pressures from abroad, thought the administration should do more to protect them from international competition, or more generously subsidize their failure to respond to it. As the recession deepened, representatives of such firms and sectors began providing money and other resources to the Democrats.

This still left the important question of devising an alternative program. Particularly given the hodgepodge of different business groups, whose power in the party was growing daily, this question had no easy answers. At the bottom of the recession, a rough compromise among different business elements within the party and the strongly protectionist AFL-CIO was worked out on "industrial policy." This committed the Democrats to offering some degree of assistance to ailing industry, while preserving the party's long term commitments to maintaining free trade. But this was hardly a bold or innovative program. And as the economy revved up again in time for the 1984 election, during the fight over the Democratic nomination various splits within the party became dramatically evident.

On the left, George McGovern and later Jesse Jackson came forward to speak for the party's mass base among poor and working Americans. Both received substantial popular support, but neither received any substantial backing from business or organized labor. In McGovern's case, a surprisingly strong showing in some of the early primaries led nowhere, and he quickly withdrew. In Jackson's, which is a special case because of its historic character, and the special position and political discipline of blacks in America, a long and often dramatic campaign staggered on through to the convention, but was also desperately constrained by a lack of resources.

On the right, a full-fledged conservative Democrat, John Glenn, emerged, promoting a program of deepening social cutbacks and further military outlays. Republican in all but name, the Glenn candidacy received massive amounts of money from business, in particular from the military sector and parts of oil, but went nowhere in the primaries.

In the center, of course, the campaign eventually shaped up as a race between Walter Mondale and Gary Hart. The latter attempted to promote a sort of high-tech version of the old New Deal program, combining a strong free trade component with virtually no commitments to labor. Elite support, in the form of contributions and advice, centered in the most "liberal" and internationally oriented business; it did not generally extend to those portions of business heavily dependent on increased domestic spending. For many downwardly mobile and highly educated "young professionals" who are overrepresented in the ranks of Democratic Party primaries, this was an attractive package, and Hart drew electoral support almost perfectly equal to Mondale.

But, especially after Glenn withdrew, Mondale became the repository for the rest of what was left of business support for the Democrats. Offering yet another conservative program, he promised a slightly lower rate of military spending than urged by Reagan, and a slightly higher rate of social spending than Hart. His preeminent issue in the general campaign, however, was the budget deficit. He proposed to address this problem, which was hardly of major salience for ordinary Americans, through a combination of spending cuts in social programs, a reduction (not reversal) of the Reagan military buildup, and substantial tax increases *without* progressive tax reform. Apart from this unexciting package, Mondale offered voters next to nothing. Despite all the talk of his close ties with labor, for example, he failed even to offer a major jobs program to deal with economic distress.

In sum, no Democrat, with the exception of McGovern and Jackson, offered a serious alternative to present policies, and they received no serious business, or even organized labor, support.

Despite this, the lesson party leaders drew from their defeat in 1984 was that the party must move further to the right, and even more closely ape Republican appeals to business. Within months of the election, the new DNC chair, Paul Kirk (considered a liberal in party circles), was quarreling openly with Lane Kirkland, and reporting to the Democratic Business Council, which he hailed as "the backbone of the Democratic Party's finances, and its intellectual resources," his progress in moving the party toward the new "political center." Not content with Kirk's efforts, a group of southern and western elected representatives established the Democratic Leadership Council to promote more conservative candidates. Alarmed, as a Kirk supporter put it, that "this group wants to take the cream of the party's leadership and leave Kirk with Jesse Jackson and the single-issue interest groups," the new DNC chair countered with his own Democratic Policy Commission, committed to similar goals. As became evident in the wide support for Gramm-Rudman, and the emergent "consensus" on removing the government of Nicaragua, the Democrats were once again prepared to move further to the right, further constraining the efforts of democratic critics of America's right turn.

4. Changing Course?
The Constraints of Present Politics

The discussion thus far indicates a variety of obstacles to democratic critics of U.S. domestic and foreign policy. These obstacles face *any* such critic. But as we noted at the outset of this discussion, we are particularly concerned with strengthening the position of critics of U.S. policies toward Central America. To conclude our discussion, then, we consider how an awareness of these constraints might inform debate within their ranks.

We should note at the outset, however, that those ranks are very diverse. What we will be calling the Central America Movement (CAM) is not really a single movement, but a convergence of diverse efforts. It is comprised of roughly 850 different support groups and organizations, operating in all 50 states. Some are affiliated with the major "solidarity" organizations—the Nicaragua Network, the Committee in Solidarity with the People of El Salvador (CISPES), and the Network in Solidarity with the People of Guatemala (NISGUA). Others are affiliated with the Pledge of Resistance, providing legislative alerts and notice of upcoming actions to the 80,000 Americans who have committed themselves to resisting the escalation of U.S. military involvement in Central America . Many work with the Sanctuary Movement; to date more than 300 churches and synagogues have declared themselves sanctuaries for Salvadoran and Guatemalan reguees, as have 21 cities and the state of New Mexico. Others have participated in the Witness for Peace program, which has led more than 80 delegations to Nicaragua in recent years, and provides an ongoing presence of U.S. observers in that country. Some have participated in the different agricultural or technical brigades that have worked in Nicaragua, or in MADRE, a "people to people" linkage of minorities and women in the U.S. and Central America. Still others are affiliated with the union-based Committee in Support of Human

Rights and Democracy in El Salvador, which is trying to break the AFL-CIO leadership's stranglehold on foreign policy actions within the labor movement. And so on.

In addition to all these groups, whose work focuses on the region, there are a number of other organizations, with broader agendas, that also work on the Central America issue. These include many elements of the religious community, including the Interreligious Task Force, and the Quest for Peace campaign; such federations as the Coalition for a New Foreign and Military Policy; elements of the Freeze movement; and such traditional peace groups as SANE.

These many different groups have different interests and agendas, and they converge only partially in their actions and beliefs on the Central America issue. What is appropriate for one group may be inappropriate for another, and our discussion here aims to respect that diversity.

This said, we turn now to five general conclusions, of relevance for the CAM, that are suggested by the previous analysis.

The Importance of Strategy

In the preceding discussion we emphasized the ways in which the fragmentation of U.S. politics erects barriers to popular politics. The existence of these barriers, in turn, leads almost naturally to a focus on achieving short term gains in particular, localized contexts. This, for example, was the strategy of collective action pursued by the American labor movement in the postwar period. At any given point, the structure of the political system makes a narrow, short term orientation seem rational, and to some degree, at any given time, it *is* rational. But almost everything we know about conventional politics also indicates that over the longer term such an orientation can be self-defeating. While it may gain temporary victories for particular groups or causes, it tends to slow coordination among groups, and to arrest any trajectory of growth for popular politics over time.

In the case of the CAM, an exclusive focus on the short term seems particularly mistaken. It seems clear, for example, that the Reagan administration (and a substantial share of Democrats as well) favors a policy of "low-intensity warfare"—using proxy forces, covert action, economic sanctions, propaganda, and so on—in Central America, and is prepared to wage such war for an *indefinite* period. For citizens of the U.S., a low intensity war obscures the consequences of U.S. interventionism, and thereby reduces the pressure to arrive at judgments, moral or otherwise, about whether interventionist policies should be pursued. It reflects the perverse political "lesson" U.S. policymakers have drawn from the experience in Vietnam— not that U.S. interventions abroad should cease, but that they should not be done with U.S. troops. But it also introduces a tremendous range of degree in the scope of U.S. involvement. By obscuring visible costs, and obscuring too the breakpoint between military intervention and diplomatic pressure, it also permits a varied and slowly escalating attack carried on over a long period. It thus buys *time*—time to enlist support for the policy at home, and to grind down those forces that might oppose it; time to suffer temporary setbacks; time to wage the sharp battles over budget and tax initiatives that have preoccupied the administration during its second term; time to move forward with the "Baker Plan" (after Treasury Secretary James Baker) to "privatize" Third World economies; time to let the dismal state of those economies, and the accumulating force of unpaid debt, increase U.S. leverage over them.

Given such long term commitments on the part of the administration, it is essential that the different elements in the CAM also position themselves for the long term.

In part this is a matter of putting things in context. No single vote in Congress—stepping up aid to the contras, or paring it down—will decide the future of Nicaragua. No single national demonstration, however attended, spells the doom or ensures the success of the CAM itself. All this is obvious, but the temptations to act as if it were not obvious—temptations produced by all the constraints enumerated here—abound. They should be resisted.

In part, however, such a long term perspective also implies that the different elements of the CAM should put a higher priority on *strategy*—on thinking through what their broad goals are, and what broad methods they will use to achieve those goals. This is, of course, easier said than done in a movement that has relatively few resources, little control over the agenda of national politics, virtually no access to the executive-centered security apparatus that initiates the policy, and no control over how nations in the region will react to those policy initiatives. To some degree, these familiar difficulties will always condemn the CAM to reacting to external events and the actions of others. But this does not defeat the point about focusing on the longer term. For without a strategic perspective, it is very difficult to make sense even of the short term, to devise coherent but flexible tactics, or to develop realistic measures of success. Without *some* view of the broad aims of the movement, it is difficult to assess the importance of electoral action, and therefore difficult to make tactical decisions about devoting scarce resources to working with elected officials. And without some view of those aims, there is no prospect of gauging the importance of grassroots work, or of making informed judgments about the specific coalitions and alliances that might help in that work. Again, of course, tactical judgments will vary. But this variation should not obscure the importance of debating and clarifying strategic questions.

All Strategies Have Costs

In some measure, discussions about strategy are already ongoing within the CAM, with different groups debating the goals of their efforts, and the tactical implications of those goals. One debate that is particularly familiar focuses on whether the general posture of the CAM should be reactive or "proactive." A closely related discussion concerns single issue mobilization versus coalitional strategies of opposition.

Some argue that the CAM must, of necessity, remain largely reactive and defensive. As the administration, supported by many Democrats, increases destructive U.S. interventions in Central America, the CAM should try to slow the rate of escalation, and prevent a military invasion. This is a reactive stance, since the terms of the CAM's activity will be defined by actors other than itself; its agenda will be set by those who make present policy. It is defensive in the sense that it aims to limit some of the worst and most obvious consequences of present policy, and not directly to mount a broader challenge to that policy. Within this generally defensive posture, moreover, it is commonly argued that the key to the CAM's success, and the most desirable strategy for it in the longer term, is to concentrate on relatively narrow issues of high salience and manifest public concern. The idea here is that by narrowing the issue around which it organizes opposition, the CAM can widen that opposition. The narrower the issue, the lighter the political "baggage" people need to carry to get on board; the more people on board, the more effective the opposition. Or so the argument goes.

Others argue—and relatively few within the CAM would dispute this—that present policies in the region are part of a more general resurgence of U.S. militarism, or, more broadly, that they are embedded in the role the U.S. has played in the world policial economy at least since World War II. It makes little sense, the argument continues, to concentrate merely on relieving some of the worst consequences of present policies; the CAM should try to change them fundamentally, and move them in a new direction. And to change policies fundamentally, of course, one has to change the basic structure of U.S. society, and the balance of political forces within it. Such an ambition naturally leads to more emphasis on alliances and coalition building between the CAM and other movements working for social justice.

There is no way the analysis of the sort offered thus far, or indeed any general political analysis, can *resolve* this complex and longstanding dispute. What can be said, however, and what might usefully inform discussions about strategy and tactics, is that all strategies have costs, and sometimes those costs are unexpected. Consider the relative merits of two broad strategies—single issue versus coalitional—just introduced. Assume for the sake of argument that the CAM reaches agreement on its short term goals. Assume too that those goals are deliberately limited—say, to blocking a direct U.S. military invasion of Nicaragua. Which strategy should be adopted?

The problems with the broad coalition strategy are, perhaps, straightforward. It would aim to prevent an invasion by advancing a comprehensive alternative to present policies. Advancing that alternative, however, would in effect require a new political vehicle—either a huge non-electoral organization, or a third party (and we have seen how difficult that is), or a massively reconstructed Democratic Party. Developing that vehicle (in whatever form) would be an extremely difficult and time consuming effort, fraught with all sorts of uncertainty, and with little chance, in the short term, of success.

Consider some of the basic requirements of such an approach. Any construction of a vehicle for a fundamental alternative to present policies would require building coalitional alliances between elements of the CAM and elements of other movements. In addition to increasing the level of mobilization around the Central America issue, the scope of mobilization would need to be extended. At a minimum, the interests of the CAM would need to be meaningfully related to those of other groups more centrally concerned about destructive U.S. policies in other regions of the world (e.g., Southern Africa or the Middle East), or at home (e.g., racial discrimination, cuts in social programs). Organizationally, this would require ongoing working relations with such groups. Working out the terms of those relations would be enormously costly and time consuming. And even if they were established, the linkage to other groups would risk a significant blurring of the Central America issue.

Given all these difficulties in a broader coalitional strategy, it might thus seem obvious that the best way to reduce U.S. violence in the region in the short run is to narrow sharply the scope of the CAM's efforts. But this is not obvious at all. By narrowing its scope, the CAM would lose the support of some people who would have joined in a more explicitly coalitional strategy. For a trade union activist with no particular concern with Central America, for example, a demand to prevent an invasion may not be an issue of great salience, even though that same activist might be prepared to support it if it were in turn joined to a program for increased jobs at home. Similarly, the intensity of commitment from individuals may be reduced. While anyone who supports a broad positive change in the direction of U.S. policies in the region, or at home, will almost surely also support a demand not to invade the region, the intensity of their commitment to this less ambitious project may be less than their commitment to an anti-invasion "plank" in a more ambitious program.

In addition to these problems of the scope and intensity of mobilization, narrower projects are typically more susceptible to disruption by shifts in tactics, or the manipulation of terms and information, by policy producers. Proponents of the nuclear freeze are familiar with the problem. With the growth in the popularity of the freeze, all manner of different proposals on strategic weapons, many of which had very little to do with actually reducing the nuclear threat, were marketed as "freeze" variations. As suggested above, the problem of shifting tactics and definitions is particularly troublesome for the CAM, however, since the administration's strategy of low intensity warfare blurs most conventional distinctions between levels of military escalation. What, for example, constitutes an invasion? Do U.S. ground troops need to be committed, or are military advisers enough? Do they need to be on the ground in the country that is the object of the attack, or can they be positioned in a neighboring country? What about a proxy invasion force, or an air war launched from Honduras? The difficulties encountered by the Pledge of Resistance (since overcome to some degree by the Pledge's focus on making the war visible, and its promotion of the Peace Alternative) in determining just when the Pledge should be called on illustrate these familiar problems of definition. But they are not, of course, merely that. They are problems of tactics and flexibility. Narrowly focused efforts risk inflexibility, and thus, especially in a fluid situation, ineffectiveness in dealing with changed tactics from the other side.

It is thus not clear, in the absence of consideration of particular cases, which strategy is better in the short term. Conversely, although we will not explore the matter at any length here, it is not clear which strategy is better in the long term. Assume for the sake of argument that the CAM reaches agreement on its long term goals. Assume too that it agrees it should seek the deep transformation of American society required for a fundamental shift in U.S. foreign policy. While it is clear that such a transformation would eventually require the mobilization of huge numbers of people over a very wide range of foreign and domestic policy concerns, it still might be true that an intense focus on the issue of Central America, as opposed to a broader focus on a range of foreign and domestic policy issues, would be a better way to *begin* such a transformation.

The point of this is not that all political judgments are equally sensible. Nor is it a perverse conclusion that narrow mobilizations are worse for short term goals, but better for long term ones. The point is simply that in debating strategies and tactics, the elements of the CAM should realize that there are always tradeoffs in those choices, always costs attached to them, and always reasonable questions that might be asked about their correctness. At a minimum, this suggests the need for toleration and openness among proponents of different views—a point we will return to below—and for the kind of flexibility emphasized earlier.

Working With the Democrats

Any political movement, even one originating outside the political mainstream, must eventually confront the question of its relations to the major parties. It must for the simple reason that those parties, however weak and disorganized they are, are *the* partisan organizations of conventional politics. Unless a movement is not interested in seeing policy results from its actions, it must at some point deal with public officials. The issue of working with the parties, then, is always one of degree and timing. How much should a strategy be oriented toward directly affecting specific legislative choices by party organizations—by seeking to elect sympathetic candidates to office, or lobbying those that are in office, or other means—and when? Because in general the Democrats still remain more accessible to critics of current policies than the Republicans, in considering this question here we confine ourselves to asking it of them. Should the CAM work with the Democratic Party?

Our analysis suggests four main points that bear on the question:

First, the question of "working with the Democratic Party" is potentially misleading. As emphasized thoughout the preceding discussion, American political parties, the Democratic Party certainly included, are relatively weak, undisciplined, and non-programmatic organizations, filled with diverse coalitions and sub-coalitions of even more diverse interests. The lack of party discipline and focus permits these coalitions to shift and reform from one issue to the next, and discourages any sharp and enduring ideological focus, even for subgroups within them. The question of working with the Democratic Party, then, is really better put as the question of working with some Democrats in some circumstances.

Second, the diversity of Democratic opinion and interest aside, it seems clear that the leading powers within the Democratic Party have shifted significantly to the right in recent years. This is not to say the Democrats, as a group, are identical to the Republicans. They are not, as the succession of votes in America's escalating war against Nicaragua indicates. Democrats initiated the major limitations on that war; they provided the chief support for those limitations; and they have led the fight against "humanitarian" and overt military aid to the contras. But the same succession of votes—culminating, as we write, with House approval of an additional $100 million aid package for the contras—indicates a willingness by many Democrats to go along with a gradual escalation of U.S. aggression toward Nicaragua. Within a set of choices about the degree of escalation, Democrats have consistently composed the ranks of those seeking to moderate that degree. But with very rare exceptions, they have not led a major fight to *reverse* the course of U.S. violence in the region, let alone contest the broader "Reagan doctrine" of Third World interventionism.

Third, this said, there are elements and individuals within the Democratic Party who have resisted its right turn, and some signs that they are seeking to consolidate their efforts. The Rainbow Coalition's national convention, and in particular the widening of its leadership structure to include representatives of organized labor and other groups, is one such sign. The new Populist Caucus, prominently featuring newly elected Senators Harkin and Simon, is another.

In addition, while it has made great gains in destroying sources of democratic resistance in America, the "Reagan revolution" has hardly solved the fundamental problems to which the right turn was a response. The U.S. continues to lose out in the race of international competition; sharp rivalries still divide the U.S. from its major allies; the devastation of Third World economies in recent years threatens even greater instability in those regions; and American elites, as ongoing conflicts over "industrial policy" make clear, are still divided over the proper allocation of costs for the reconstruction of the American economy.

Within such an environment of uncertainty and change, the importance of politics is manifestly heightened. And while divisions among elites hardly guarantee gains by those beneath them, they may permit gains in particular circumstances. As it looks to gain a toehold for resistance against present policies, it would be foolish of the CAM to ignore existing forms of resistance within Democratic ranks. There is surely no reason for thinking that working with the Democrats provides *the* key to changing the course of present policies. Equally surely, however, there is no *principle* that bars working with any Democrats, on any aspects of the issue, at any time.

Fourth, the real issue then, is not whether the CAM should ever work with the Democrats, but under what conditions it might work with some of them; and the answer turns on what the terms of exchange, or the rules on working together, are. Politicians are notoriously fickle, a fickleness encouraged in the U.S. by the weakness of party structures. The CAM does not, in general, have the power to discipline and punish those who lie to it. And given this position of relative weakness, it would be unreasonable for the CAM to seek to increase its own power merely by increasing the power of those whom it believed to be "sympathetic." Such "bootstrap" operations seldom work, and can easily backfire in disastrous ways. They can, for example, squander resources with no gain at all, or kill independent organizations by turning them into instruments of someone else's political ambition. This is one of the many lessons to be drawn from the alliance between American labor and the Democratic Party—an alliance that benefitted one of the participants far more than the other. The CAM should learn that lesson, recognize its own limits, and, critically, be clear on what *it* wishes to achieve in specific working relations.

This last point can be put another way. It is sometimes implied in discussions of working with, or within, the Democratic Party, that the preeminent goal of a social movement should be "access." This seems patently wrong. There is always a price for access, and if the price rises, say, to the level of a gag rule on demands by that movement once it has access, then the price is obviously too high, and the effort is self-defeating.

The Importance of An Alternative

We have noted at several points that the strategic and tactical judgments of different elements within the CAM will differ, and that no analysis can change that fact, or pretend to resolve those differences completely. But all of the preceding discussion has also underscored the disastrous consequences of fragmentation within popular politics. It follows from the analysis that the different elements of the CAM, despite their diversity, should wherever possible seek to coordinate their activities.

Ideally, any framework of cooperation among the different elements of the CAM should take an *organized* form—presumably of a coalitional, and not a highly hierarchical sort. Gestures in the direction of such organization should be encouraged. But respect for the profound ideological diversity of the movement, its decentralization, and its lack of resources, underscores the difficulties of constructing such an organization. Even if seriously attempted, it seems unlikely to reach completion in the near term.

But there is an intermediate level of coordination, compatible both with a higher level of organization, and the present diversity of the CAM, that is possible. That is the articulation and promotion of a framework of general principles for U.S. foreign policy and, based on those principles, the outlines for an alternative U.S. policy toward the Central America and the Caribbean region. The PACCA Peace Alternative, based on proposals in PACCA's *Changing Course*, is one such framework. It argues from basic principles that PACCA believes should govern U.S. relations with the region—nonintervention, a respect for the self-determination of other peoples, collective self-defense, peaceful settlement of disputes, the encouragement of human rights and democracy, compatibility between foreign and domestic policy values, and support for equity and development—to some two dozen specific recommendations for specific changes in present U.S. policies there—including such recommendations as ending U.S. military exercises in the region, dismantling U.S. bases in Honduras, lifting the economic boycott of Cuba, and promoting regional economic development.[22]

This is not the place to defend this particular policy alternative. What we do wish to argue for, however, is the desirability of promoting *some* such alternative as a form of linkage among the different elements of the CAM. We see four good reasons for making such an effort.

First, the CAM, and those critical of U.S. policies elsewhere, are commonly accused of only being "negative," of not having anything positive to say about the policies they support. A positive alternative meets this objection head on, and its active promotion would provide CAM activists with the confidence that comes from being able to meet the objection. Of course it might be further objected that any serious alternative is "impractical"—meaning that given the present array of forces in American politics it could not be implemented immediately. But this "practicality" objection really just amounts to a political objection. If a proposal's "practicality" turns on its being susceptible to implementation by present political forces, then *any* radical departure from present policies can be seen as "impractical," and the charge of impracticality only amounts to an announcement of political disagreement. The CAM should not be troubled by such objections, particularly if its time horizons are stretched beyond the short term. And in any case, pressing into focus just why a sound and just alternative would be resisted, and just what the objections to it are, would be revealing in itself.

Second, among the different elements of the CAM, a positive alternative could provide a broad framework of common conviction that would ease coalitional alliances. Agreement among different groups about an alternative, itself a unifying action, would go some distance to relieving the strains of difference that remain. Remaining differences can be better handled if they can be articulated against a background of explicit agreement on *something*. Thus an alternative may help the different ambitions of the CAM cohere, giving the CAM as a whole greater integrity and focus. That integrity and focus, in turn, would permit greater tactical flexibility.

Third, agreement on an alternative can ease the CAM's relations with other movements and groups. At some level of generality, everyone honestly concerned about social justice, either at home or abroad, already enjoys some level of agreement. The problem is that it is difficult to translate that vague general agreement into more concrete working relations. Stating an alternative based on shared principles helps address this problem by establishing an intermediate frame of reference and discussion—more abstract than the rules governing day-to-day cooperation, but much more concrete than vague statements of concern.

Fourth and finally, merely stating an alternative vision of policy, and working through the details of what it might look like, makes a change in present policies more imaginable for people. This applies within the CAM, and to other democratic movements, but it applies with special force to those who object to present policies, but do not act on those objections. An alternative, in short, is a good organizing tool for the CAM to use in widening its audience, and its membership, beyond existing activists and supporters.

Attitudes

Finally, the preceding discussion may indicate something about the attitude that critics of U.S. policies in Central American should take toward themselves, and one another. We enter two points here.

First, as emphasized throughout, politics *is* hard, and popular democratic politics is harder still. As we have argued at some length, the political environment within which the CAM operates throws up countless obstacles to its success. These are the basic rules of the game of American politics, and they are reflected in the uncertain progress of the CAM thus far. But recognizing the existence of these obstacles and constraints has an important corollary: While there are, no doubt, any number of mistakes that critics of U.S. policies in Central America have made, and no doubt much room for improvement in their coordination, their strategy, and their tactics, they should resist *blaming* themselves for all the difficulties of opposition. They did not invent the game of American politics. They only, acting on moral and political principles, condemned themselves to playing it.

Second, we have argued that many of the strategic and tactical choices that the different groups in the CAM debate—from the wisdom of single issue mobilization versus coalition building, to working with or without the Democratic Party—cannot be decided at the level of political principle. It follows that they should not be made into matters of principle, and used to excoriate or accuse one another. They should be recognized as matters on which reasonable and honest people can and will disagree. This promises to be a long war, and differences within the CAM will continue through its course. But for all their disagreements, the different elements within the CAM do share an important commitment that sets them apart from the makers of current policy. They are committed to the democratic ideal that other nations and peoples of the world should be treated with respect. Practicing democratic values of mutual respect and tolerance within the CAM itself is a natural, and necessary, extension of that commitment.

Notes

1. See the review of recent trends in public opinion in Thomas Ferguson and Joel Rogers, *Right Turn: The Decline of the Democrats and the Future of American Politics* (New York: Hill & Wang, 1986), chapter 1.

2. See, for example, the *New York Times*/CBS News Poll reported in *New York Times*, 15 April 1986, A6. It shows 62 percent of Americans opposed to giving further aid to the contra rebels, with only 25 percent supporting President Reagan's recent request for an additional $100 million in funding. Strikingly, 52 percent of those who approve of Reagan's handling of the presidency also oppose increased aid.

3. For a general analysis of the fragmenting tendencies of American politics, on which we draw here, see Walter Dean Burnham, "The United States: The Politics of Heterogeneity," in *Electoral Behavior: A Comparative Handbook*, ed. Richard Rose (New York: Free Press, 1974), 653-725. Burnham's essay is probably the best single statement of the ways in which "American exceptionalism" is produced and reflected throughout the political system.

4. Alexander Hamilton, James Madison, and John Jay, *The Federalist Papers* (New York: Mentor, 1961), 79.

5. *Federalist Papers*, 81.

6. See the discussion in Burnham, "Politics of Heterogeneity," which emphasizes this as the basis of much ethnic politics in the U.S.

7. Werner Sombart, *Why is there no Socialism in the United States?* (White Plains, NY: M.E. Sharpe, 1976), 106. Sombart's work was originally published in 1906. For the classic modern version of this argument, see David Potter, *People of Plenty: Economic Abundance and the American Character* (Chicago: University of Chicago Press, 1954).

8. For a short, seminal treatment of the Civil War, see Barrington Moore, Jr., *Social Origins of Dictatorship and Democracy* (Boston: Beacon Press, 1967), chapter 3. On the Populists, see Lawrence Goodwyn, *Democratic Promise: The Populist Moment in America* (New York: Oxford University Press, 1976). Always intertwined with the issue of race, the sources and fate of populism in the South are particularly important to understanding that region's political underdevelopment. Among recent studies, see Steven Hahn, *The Roots of Southern Populism: Yeoman Farmers and the Transformation of the Georgia Upcountry, 1850-1890* (New York: Oxford University Press, 1983).

9. *Statistical Abstract*, Tables 2, 127.

10. A useful recent discussion of the interaction of religion and class in the 19th century (and beyond) is provided in Mike Davis, *Prisoners of the American Dream* (London: Verson, 1986).

11. See, however, the ambitious attempt to chronicle part of this history in Robert Justin Goldstein, *Political Repression in Modern America: From 1870 to the Present* (Cambridge, MA: Schenkman, 1978).

12. The notion of "rational ignorance" is explored in Anthony Downs, *An Economic Theory of Democracy* (New York: Harper & Row, 1957). For other difficulties of collective action, see the seminal work by Mancur Olson, *The Logic of Collective Action: Public Goods and the Theory of Groups* (Cambridge, MA: Harvard University Press, 1965). Notice that we are assuming here that people behave in "economically rational" ways, that is, that they only engage in those actions the marginal return on which is greater than the marginal cost. It is possible to embrace this view as a guide to political action within capitalist democracies without commiting to the broader claims about human motivation typically made by neoclassical economists. For an exposition of this point, see Joshua Cohen and Joel Rogers, *On Democracy* (New York: Penguin, 1983), chapter 3.

13. For comparative rates of unionization in the U.S. and Western Europe, current as of 1978, see U.S. Department of Labor, Office of Foreign Economic Research, *Report of the President on U.S. Competitiveness*, September 1980, Table V 27. Because of differences in background legislation and measurement techniques, international comparisons in this area are especially tricky. For a recent review of the data, and a guide to the difficulties, see Jelle Visser, "Dimensions of Union Growth in Postwar Western Europe," European University Institute, Working Paper # 89, Florence, February 1984. For the most recent figures on U.S. unions density, see Larry T. Adams, "Union Membership of Employed Wage and Salary Workers," *Current Wage Developments*, March 1986, 45.

14. McCarthy offers an account of the difficulties he had in 1976 in getting on the ballot in his *The Ultimate Tyranny* (New York: Harcourt Brace Jovanovich, 1980).

15. Walter Dean Burnham, "The 1984 Election and the Future of American Politics," in *Election '84: Landslide without a Mandate?*, ed. Ellis

Sandoz and Cecil V. Crabb, Jr. (New York: New American Library, 1985), 215.

16. Walter Dean Burnham, *The Current Crisis in American Politics* (New York: Oxford University Press, 1982), 124. 17.

17. The language of "appearance" and "disappearance," and much of the analysis that follows, is drawn from Walter Dean Burnham. See his "The Appearance and Disappearance of the American Voter," in *Current Crisis,* 121-65.

18. For an analysis of the New Deal that is particularly attentive to the sources of business support for it, see Thomas Ferguson, "From Normalcy to New Deal: Industrial Structure, Party Competition, and American Public Policy in the Great Depression," *International Organization* 38 (1984): 41-94.

19. For one overview of the operation of the consolidated New Deal system in the postwar period, see Cohen and Rogers, *On Democracy,* chapter 4.

20. The analysis in this and the following section draws heavily on Ferguson and Rogers, *Right Turn,* chapters 3, 5, and 6.

21. See footnote 1, above.

22. See PACCA, *Changing Course: Blueprint for Peace in Central America and the Caribbean* (Washington, DC: Institute for Policy Studies, 1984).

RESOURCES

1. For information on the federal budget and Central America contact the institutions affiliated with Policy Alternatives for the Caribbean and Central America.

    Center for the Study of the Americas
    2288 Fulton Street, #103
    Berkeley, CA 94704
    (415) 540-5006

    Central America Resource Center
    P.O. Box 2327
    Austin, TX 78768
    (512) 476-9841

    Institute for Food and Development Policy
    1885 Mission Street
    San Francisco, CA 94103
    (415) 864-8555

    Institute for Policy Studies
    1901 Q Street NW
    Washington DC 20009
    (202) 234-9382

    North American Congress on Latin America
    151 W. 19th Street
    New York NY 10011
    (212) 989-8890

2. Solidarity Networks: These networks can refer you to regional centers for further information.

    Committee in Solidarity with the People of El Salvador
    Box 50139
    Washington DC 20004
    (202) 393-3370

    National Network in Solidarity with the Nicaraguan People
    2025 Eye Stree NW, Suite 1117
    Washington DC 20006
    (202) 223-2328

    Network in Solidarity with the People of Guatemala
    930 F Street NW, Suite 720
    Washington DC 20004
    (202) 483-0050

3. Religious Networks: The task forces listed below provide resources and listings of Protestant, Jewish, and Catholic local affiliates across the U.S.

    Inter-Religious Task Force
    475 Riverside Drive, Room 633
    New York, NY 10015
    (212) 870-3383

New Jewish Agenda
149 Church Street, #2N
New York, NY 10007
(212) 227-5885

Religious Task Force on Central America
1747 Connecticut Avenue NW
Washington DC 20009
(202) 387-7652

4. For additional resources on Central America, contact:

American Friends Service Committee
National Action/Research on the Military Industrial Complex
1501 Cherry Street
Philadelphia, PA 19102
(215) 241-7175

Center for Defense Information
1500 Massachusetts Avenue NW
Washington DC 20002
(202) 862-0700

Center for International Policy
120 Maryland Avenue NE
Washington DC 20002
(202) 544-4666

Central America Historical Institute
Intercultural Center
Georgetown University
Washington DC 20057

Central America Research Institute
P.O. Box 4797
Berkeley, CA 94704
(415) 843-5041

Clergy and Laity Concerned
198 Broadway
New York, NY 10038
(212) 964-6730

Council on Hemispheric Affairs
1612 20th Street NW
Washington DC 20009
(202) 745-7000

Ecumenical Program for Interamerican Communication and
   Action (EPICA)
1470 Irving Street NW
Washington DC 20010
(202) 332-0292

Honduras Information Center
1 Summer Street
Somerville, MA 02143
(617) 625-7220

International Center for Development Policy
731 8th Street SE
Washington DC 20003
(202) 547-3800

MADRE
853 Broadway, Room 905
New York, NY 10003
(212) 777-6470

National Central America Health Rights Network
853 Broadway, Suite 1105
New York, NY 10003
(212) 420-9635

National Labor Committe in Support of Democracy and Human Rights in El Salvador
15 Union Square
New York, NY 10003
(212) 242-0700

Office Of the Americas
1227 4th Street
Santa Monica, CA 90401
(213) 451-2428

Pledge of Resistance
P.O. Box 53411
Washington DC 20009
(202) 328-4040

The Quixote Center
P.O. Box 5206
Hyattsville, MD 20782
(301) 699-0042

The Resource Center
P.O. Box 4726
Albuquerque, NM 87102
(505) 266-5009

Washington Office on Latin America
110 Maryland Avenue NE
Washington DC 20002
(202) 544-8045

Women's Coalition to Stop U.S. Intervention in Central America and the Caribbean
475 Riverside Drive, Room 812
New York, NY 10115
(212) 870-2359

OTHER PACCA PUBLICATIONS

Inequity and Intervention
Part of the Domestic Roots Series, this pamphlet explores the budgetary impact of the Reagan administration's Central America strategy, and the overall cost of an interventionist foreign policy, drawing the connection between high military outlays and cuts in social spending.
South End Press, 1986, $4.75

Transition and Development: Problems of Third World Socialism
A critical examination of the problems encountered when Third World countries attempt a socialist transformation to alleviate poverty and repression.
Monthly Review Press, 1986, $11.00

Changing Course: Blueprint for Peace in Central America
An outline for U.S. policy in the region which continues to be used as a basis for peace alternatives.
Institute for Policy Studies, $5.00
An accompanying study guide is available for 50 cents.

Joshua Cohen is an associate professor of philosophy and political science at the Massachusetts Institute of Technology. Joel Rogers is an associate professor of law at the University of Miami. They are co-authors of **On Democracy** and **Inequity and Intervention**.

A timely analysis which explores why the basic structure of American politics keeps people divided, and how organization and citizens' alternatives can bring us back together.

—Jesse Jackson
President, Rainbow Coalition

Will be read and studied by the new generation of progressive leaders.

—Heather Booth
Program Director, Citizen Action

Rules of the Game offers important insights for those attempting to return a greater share of economic and political power to average Americans.

—Representative Lane Evans, D-Ill.
Chairman, Congressional Populist Caucus

A lucid and concise handbook on U.S. political structure and parties.

—Francis Farenthold
Co-Founder, Women's Political Caucus

This pamphlet will help in the peace community's fight to close the gap and make U.S. policy reflect the wishes of the majority of Americans.

—David Cortright
Executive Director, SANE

An essential handbook for every grassroots organizer, **Rules of the Game** poses a difficult, but crucial question faced by all of us: how can we make an increasing impact on our country's political processes?

—Angela Sanbrano, national coordinator of CISPES
—Jo Ann Heisel, national coordinator of NISGUA
—Debra Reuben, national coordinator of NNSNP

PACCA's **Rules of the Game** makes important strides toward clarifying how and when the anti-intervention movement can work through conventional political channels.

—David Reed
Executive Director, Coalition for a New Foreign and Military Policy

Rules of the Game offers an enlightening historical perspective and timely structural analysis for understanding the American political system.

—Andrea Kydd
Executive Director, the Youth Project

SOUTH END PRESS

$5.00
cover design by Mike Prokosch

International/Political Science
0-89608-326-8